D0463927

The Modern
Irish Writers

The Modern Irish Writers

Cross Currents of Criticism

by

Estella Ruth Taylor

GREENWOOD PRESS, PUBLISHERS
WESTPORT, CONNECTICUT

The Library of Congress cataloged this book as follows:

Taylor, Estella Ruth.
The modern Irish writers; cross currents of criticism.
New York, Greenwood Press [1969, °1954]

176 p.   23 cm.

Bibliographical references included in "Notes" (p. 143–165) Bibliography: p. 166–170.

1. Irish literature (English)—History and criticism.   2. English literature—Irish authors—History and criticism.   3. Criticism—Ireland.   I. Title.

PR8753.T3   1969   820.9   69–14108

Library of Congress   [3]

Reprinted with the permission of the University of Kansas Press

Reprinted in 1969 by Greenwood Press, a division of Congressional Information Service, Inc.,
51 Riverside Avenue, Westport, Connecticut 06880

Library of Congress catalog card number 69-14108
ISBN 0-8371-0678-8

Printed in the United States of America

10 9 8 7 6 5 4 3 2

TO

WILLIAM FRANK BRYAN

ACKNOWLEDGMENTS

There is only one way by which the fruits of research done in contemporary writers can be properly shared, and that is by the cordial co-operation of those organizations and persons who hold the copyrights to the works drawn upon. Hence, for permission to quote copyrighted material, I am greatly indebted to the following: *The Commonweal;* Dodd, Mead and Co.; Duell, Sloan & Pearce, Inc.; The Educational Company of Ireland, Ltd.; Funk and Wagnalls Company; Victor Gollancz, Ltd.; Harcourt, Brace and Company, Inc.; Henry Holt and Company, Inc.; Hodges, Figgis & Co., Ltd.; Little, Brown & Company; Liveright Publishing Corporation; Longmans, Green & Co., Inc.; The Macmillan Company; *The Nation,* Thomas Nelson & Sons; New Directions; Oxford University Press; G. P. Putnam's Sons; Random House, Inc.; Survey Associates, Inc.; The Talbot Press Limited; The Viking Press Inc.; *The Yale Review,* copyright Yale University Press.

I am indebted personally to Oliver St. John Gogarty, Professor Denis Gwyn, St. John Ervine, Frank O'Connor, and C. D. Medley, to the latter of whom George Moore bequeathed the copyright to *A Mummer's Wife,* for permission to quote, and to L. S. Gógan, of the National Museum of Ireland, for his informative comments, which are recorded in my explanatory notes. I most gratefully acknowledge the help of Professors Arthur H. Nethercot and Moody E. Prior, who read my manuscript and gave me helpful advice during the course of my study of the modern Irish writers. I wish, also, to express my sincere appreciation for the counsel and direction given by the Editor of the University of Kansas Press during his careful editing of the text and notes of this book.

E. R. T.

CONTENTS

The Modern
Irish Writers

INTRODUCTION

Much has been written about the school of modern Irish writers whose activities were centered in Dublin during the nineties and the first four decades of the twentieth century, and biographies of the chief participants in the Irish literary revival have been provided, but one approach to these writers has been overlooked,—namely, the gathering together of their scattered statements of opinion, and their reflections and self-evaluations, which form a body of criticism distinguished by its highly personal and self-conscious tone.

As late as 1931 Daniel Corkery in the preface to his book, *Synge and Anglo-Irish Literature,* complained that the criticism by which Anglo-Irish literature is assessed is neither Irish nor Anglo-Irish: "The typical Irish expatriate writer continues to find his matter in Irish life. . . . Anglo-Irish literature then, as the phrase is understood, is mostly the product of Irishmen who neither live at home nor write primarily for their own people. Furthermore, the criticism by which it is assessed is not Irish, nor even Anglo-Irish."[1] On the contrary, the Irish writers who have not been consciously evaluating their literature coincident with creating it are few, and one of the most characteristic features of the Dublin school is that its members were constantly carrying on a two-way activity, simultaneously producing literature and sitting in judgment on their peers. Not only has the modern Irish writer tended to reveal himself autobiographically very soon after his initial success, writing, as it were, his apologia before he has had a great deal in print to defend, but he has also been prodigal of comment upon his associates, in magazine articles and in the prefaces to the plays and other printed works of his contemporaries, and has freely interspersed pages of literary criticism in many divergent forms, such as, for example, the travelogue and the sportsman's essay, as in Padraic Colum's *The Road Round Ireland* and in Lord Dunsany's *My Ireland,* respectively. Moreover, he has frequently used his contemporary craftsmen as the subjects of his fictional expression, thereby establishing a vogue for what becomes, in effect, an implied criticism.

Closely associated with these writers were numerous contributors to English and American, as well as to Irish, periodicals, who, being Irish themselves, showed an exceptional interest in every detail of the personality and output of the dramatists, poets, and novelists of their homeland, and who served to increase the public interest in the Celtic movement in literature. In short, there exists an extensive and valuable body of critical comment from the pens of Irish authors: from those who remained in their native country and looked upon themselves at close range, and from those who, having become voluntary exiles, looked back more objectively, perhaps, upon the locale and the artists who frequented it either continuously or intermittently.

This criticism varies in quality, extending from the most caustic personal comment, which, in many cases, is obviously generated by a spirit of rivalry or jealousy, to the most carefully considered evaluations of the writers' philosophies and individual works. Although this large body of criticism is widely scattered in point of time and place of publication, there are certain recurring strands of thought running through the whole of it which form clearly distinguishable patterns. For instance, a frequent approach to any writer is through the definition of the typical Irish character and of the Irish mind, with the subsequent application of the definition to the individual author as a unit of measurement in determining the validity of the writer's expression. In the traditional fashion, the critic takes into account the religion and politics of his author in order to show the effects of the author's religious training, or of his political alignment, upon his work. The problems of Gaelic and the dialects occupied the attention of the critic from the beginning. Everywhere are to be found the testimonies of the participants in the literary quarrels, which arose as frequently out of natural antipathies felt by members of the group as out of occasion or incident. And, finally, the writer analyzes the literary theories and the underlying philosophies of his contemporaries and pronounces

4

judgment upon the actual and probable influence of each writer as a producer of poems, plays, essays, and novels.

It is my intention to demonstrate that the Irish frequently referred to themselves as a school with certain specified centers of social repartee; a school with avowed aims and purposes which were sometimes subject to dispute within the membership; a school with organizations functioning for the pleasure and improvement of the Irish public and for the fostering of literary and dramatic genius. I shall then deal with the Irish critics' observations and reports of the various attitudes of the writers who compose this school, with the emphasis falling upon the opinions of those who were simultaneously critics and practitioners in the literary arts. The reader will keep in mind that "for the most part the critics were the poets and the poets were the critics."[2]

The members of this modern Irish school of writers were for a period of fifty years actively engaged in criticism as well as in creative writing. Their criticism showed a sensitive awareness of race and homeland which led them to make repeated attempts at analysis of the Irish mind. They were constantly looking for the Celtic element in the writings of their associates and holding their contemporaries up to judgment in the light of their Irish authenticity. They were likewise keenly aware of their neighbors, the English, whether resident in Ireland or at home in England, and held them in respect because of their cultural gifts. They accepted the English language as their mother tongue and showed little sympathy with the exaggerated demands of the supporters of Gaelic.

The writers of the Irish school, while evaluating themselves as the exponents of a literary renaissance, were prone to give exaggerated praise. In their day-to-day associations they ran into conflicts which prompted public utterance of a wholly reverse nature. In this personal stock-taking they have set down detailed pictures that leave a vivid impression of both the person and character of the Irish writers.

Their criticism took cognizance of the underlying principles which motivated their artistic production. They have left acknowledgments of reciprocal influences and have made

5

prophecies regarding the probable outward extensions of those influences in time and space.

The sum and substance of the critique leaves the student of Irish letters convinced that here is a group at once homogeneous and yet engaged in some conflict—a conflict essential to a live society of artists. Whatever may have been said to the contrary, the Irish writers have been submitted to the judgment of their peers, and by that judgment have achieved distinction over and above that which their creative works alone merit.

"A normal literature," writes Daniel Corkery, "while welcoming the criticism of outsiders neither lives nor dies by such criticism. It abides the judgement of its own people, and by that judgement lives or dies."[3]

Chapter I

THE TYPICAL MANIFESTATIONS OF A SCHOOL

1. The Coterie

There was a central coterie among the modern Irish writers, who early established the fact that they looked upon themselves as a school, although more than one of their contemporaries among the Irish and the English have explicitly denied to them sufficient cohesion of purpose to entitle them to any such claim.[1] George Moore, who has given us the most celebrated, though probably not the most accurate, of all the treatments of the men and women who were engaged in the reform of Irish literature, records their recognition of themselves as a coterie who were consciously endeavoring to build a new Ireland intellectually and politically worthy of all the sufferings that every class and creed had endured in the past.[2] Padraic Colum also recognized this coterie as rising after the downfall of Parnell. He described the group as one in which a homogeneous and enthusiastic leadership prevailed in spite of the fact that everybody knew everyone else's foibles and oddities.[3]

Who, then, were those who felt the obligation to build a new Ireland? Who may properly be considered members of the Dublin school? Where do we draw the line of exclusion? Who are within the pale, and who stand independently without? And what have they themselves declared to be their purposes?

As a matter of fact, there were circles within circles, concentric, eccentric, and overlapping. As the wheel turned and gained momentum, a few on the outer rim were thrown off and never re-established a personal connection. All those who were participants in the theatre movement, either as writers of or producers of plays, all the members of the Irish Academy of Letters, and all those who with regular frequency met together informally for literary repartee have voice in this interplay of criticism. They may be considered in one of two categories, either as the creative writers, who were also the movers and instigators of artistic fulfillment, or as the journalistic spectators and reporters of the doings and sayings of the creative members.

If one were to set down merely those names which appeared on that unique social register, the great copper beech in Lady Gregory's garden at Coole, he would have the roll of the prime movers, the central coterie. But the larger circles include the membership of the Academy, some of whom were journalists by profession, and, as previously suggested, those connected with the Abbey Theatre at one time or another. Such connections entitle one to be heard wherever Irish comment upon Irish literature leads to a final decree. Beyond the core, comprised of William Butler Yeats, George William Russell (A. E.),[4] John Millington Synge, Lady Augusta Gregory, George Moore, Edward Martyn, and Douglas Hyde, there appear in the second circle Padraic Colum, James Stephens, William Kirkpatrick Magee (John Eglinton),[5] Lord Dunsany, Stephen MacKenna, and Oliver St. John Gogarty. As the circle expands, Lennox Robinson, Stephen Gwynn, Denis Gwynn, L. A. G. Strong, St. John Ervine, E. A. Boyd, Frank O'Connor, Susan Mitchell, Daniel Corkery, Darrell Figgis, and A. E. Malone are drawn within its sphere.[6]

At the dawn of the awakening stands Katharine Tynan,[7] who was well aware of what forces were shaping things to come in the literary world of Dublin, but whose own work is distinctly allied to that of the English Victorians. Stephen Gwynn establishes her relationship to the Irish school. It will be noted that he draws this distinction, that she was never self-consciously Irish: "In so far as the creation of a distinctive Irish literature was organized and worked for, she [Katharine Tynan] never belonged to the movement. Yet appearing when it did, her work strengthened the movement. In it Ireland had something to show, not the less Irish because it was never self-consciously Irish; something Irish because it could be no other."[8] Her critical comment, while distinctly feminine in character, and rather more sentimentally reminiscent than logically disinterested, will, nevertheless, be taken into account as adding that detail which offers at times a clue to a fuller comprehension.

James Joyce stands somewhat apart from the other members of the school for the reason that, as an expatriate, he did little or nothing to foster even the most tenuous of personal relationships with his Irish contemporaries. There is less cross-comment between him, whose view was universal, and the Dubliners who remained more provincial, than was circulated constantly in critical exchange among those who were in more continuous contact in Ireland. His work is, however, paramount in the study of the city, the atmosphere, the milieu in which the work of all the others was largely done. It is not necessary here to acknowledge the greater magnitude of his genius nor the more distant extensions of his influence. Stephen Gwynn credits him with recalling the Dublin scene: "Dublin of these years [early years of the Abbey plays] is recalled to us in part by George Moore, but far more intimately by James Joyce, in his *Portrait of the Artist as a Young Man*, which describes the student life. We can learn there that lines from Yeats haunted the young men—not recalled as ringing phrases that prompted action, but simply as melodies filling the mind with high and delicate beauty."[9]

That Joyce himself felt no allegiance to the group no one will deny. Padraic Colum notes the fact in *The Road Round Ireland:* "He talked of Ibsen on the night I first spoke to him . . . . The Irish Revival had no allegiance from him—he distrusted all enthusiasm, he said. The prospect of creating a national theater was already discounted by him."[10] Charles Duff sees in Joyce the personalization of the reaction to the school: "We often see it stated that Joyce is one of the figures thrown up by the Irish literary revival, but this is true only in the sense that he was a reaction *against* it. It is entirely erroneous to associate him in any other way with the general tendencies shown in the work of contemporary Irishmen, most of which was propagandist and therefore contrary to his whole conception of art."[11]

No one who has read *Ulysses* can accuse Joyce of indifference, however, although he may agree that Joyce felt no allegiance to, and is in practice wholly divergent from, the literary aims of that coterie who formed the nucleus of literary life in Dublin.

The recognition of Yeats and A. E. as leaders of a school may be found with monotonous regularity, but perhaps is nowhere more singularly expressed than by Darrell Figgis, who calls them "apostles" while he is distinguishing them as "conductors" of the revival:

What was called the "Irish Literary Revival" was truly an English literary revival conducted by Irishmen. In this W. B. Yeats had a conscious part; but A. E. was rather caught into it from his own separate world, that was only literary in the sense that to convey spiritual experiences from soul to soul was to put them into writing, and that to convey them justly was to write them finely, with a commensurate music and imagination. W. B. Yeats' apostleship was designed and deliberate, and the immediate results were excellent though the work became spoiled in time; but A. E. was rather an unsuspecting apostle, a little bewildered in the white light of publicity that had so suddenly fallen about him in his emergence from the household in Ely Place.[12]

Darrell Figgis, after speaking of A. E.'s life of mystical experience and experiment, of his study of the writings of the ancient seers, of his habits of contemplation and meditation, defines his place in the school—"that very rare circle of friendship that became, before its members were scattered through the world, almost a community of mind"—as that of "almost a spiritual dictatorship."[13]

As one explores the criticism of the modern Irish writers by their fellow-Irish, he soon finds conflict of opinion as to who was the actual founder of this or that society, the strongest influence upon a particular genius, or even the founder of the Gaelic League or the Abbey Theatre. Denis Gwynn is as ardent a champion of Edward Martyn as a leader as Figgis is of A. E., disputing the generally accepted view that Yeats and Lady Gregory were the "primum mobile" as far as the Literary Theatre is concerned. Gwynn would even have us feel that

No other Irishman, in the various movements which together may be generally described as the 'Irish Revival'—between the eighteen-nineties and the establishment of the Irish Free State in 1921—occupies the same prominent place as Edward Martyn as a connecting link between so many intellectual activities . . . . He had already made a reputation among men of letters when Mr. W. B. Yeats was beginning to be known as a poet; and it was he who introduced Mr. Yeats to both Mr. George Moore and to Lady Gregory and obtained their collaboration with him in founding the Irish Literary Theatre. It was Edward Martyn who not only provided the money with which the first group of actors were got together, but who also wrote the first play which attracted favorable attention when it was acted in Dublin, and so made the subsequent development possible.[14]

Gwynn shows some resentment over the brevity of Yeats' acknowledgment before the Swedish Royal Academy of Martyn's part in the founding of the Irish Literary Theatre and adds that Yeats' account in his book is an incomplete version: "The Irish Literary Theatre, and the Abbey Theatre which arose from its early beginnings would never have come into existence if it had not been for the public spirit and the enthusiasm of Edward Martyn, who is dismissed with this melancholy gesture of condescension. And although quite a number of large books have been written concerning the modern Irish drama, the story remains curiously unconvincing without any full record of Edward Martyn's own part in bringing it to life."[15]

Gwynn denounces Lady Gregory more specifically than by merely alluding to "a number of large books." He complained that in her book on the Irish theatre she leaves the impression that at the time of her meeting with Yeats at Comte de Bosterot's, where they laid the ground plan for the theatre, Edward Martyn was by mere chance paying a call, there being no indication of the fact that the Comte was Edward's cousin and most intimate friend. By this curiously extraneous detail he seeks to establish that Lady Gregory failed to give credit where credit was due.

Martyn's own statement, provided us in a manuscript left by Martyn to his literary executor, Denis Gwynn, and now in

11

print in Gwynn's life of Martyn, shows a little testiness that hints at underlying temperamental differences.[16] Surely Martyn stands alone in his reference to *Cathleen ni Houlihan* as "a silly little play." It is clear that Martyn looks cynically at the Abbey and feels his isolation:

We all know how useless it is to push a person without talent . . . . These are the sort of persons, however, whom Mr. Yeats and Lady Gregory triumphantly succeeded in pushing . . . . He proclaimed their merits in his most dictatorial vein until they actually got to believe in themselves and even to show signs of some improvement. Meanwhile the mediocrities taking their cue from the dictator went about fussing over the art of those players until they made them notorious enough to attract silly little people with silly little plays like *Cathleen ni Houlihan* and *The Pot of Broth* to the amused surprise of those who were in the habit of thinking for themselves.[17]

Martyn said, frankly, that he himself could not write peasant plays, for the simple reason that they did not interest him, and that because he did not furnish such plays for the Abbey Theatre, he became an isolated figure. He criticized the Abbey players for limiting their acting powers, declaring that they had confined themselves to the acting of peasant and middle class roles until they had become totally unfitted to portray the upper classes.[18]

Whatever the merits of the case may be (and the claims of Lady Gregory and Yeats are too widely supported to need defense here), it is well enough understood that Martyn did belong to the inner circle, and he has the unenviable distinction of having drawn more comment from George Moore than any other writer of the period. It was Moore who said in *Hail and Farewell* that Martyn had telegraphed him, "The sceptre of intelligence has passed from London to Dublin."[19] But Yeats says in *Dramatis Personae* that that sounds more like Moore than like the "economical tongue-tied Martyn."[20]

Colum claims Lord Dunsany for the movement, and by virtue of the pertinent comment that Dunsany has made upon his contemporaries as well as for the fact that four of his plays were produced at the Abbey, his attitudes should be taken into account. Colum has said that although Dunsany never used an Irish name in any of his plays or stories, he was, nevertheless, under the influence of the Irish literary movement.[21] Dunsany himself was proud to be of the company. In his memoirs he refers to the pride he felt in having one of his early stories, "Time and the Gods," included in *The Shenachie,* a magazine which published in the same issue "charming tales" by Bernard Shaw and George Moore.[22]

The connections of Douglas Hyde were almost wholly centered in the Gaelic League, and critical references to him in that relationship abound. Since all members of the school were acutely aware of the problems raised by the Nationalists' language movement, a study of their reflections upon the significance of Gaelic demands a separate treatment. In a subsequent chapter dealing with this phase of the modern Irish writers' activity, Douglas Hyde's place in the coterie will be clearly established.

James Stephens was brought into the coterie by A. E., whose satisfaction in his protégé seems to have annoyed Yeats to such a degree that he was tardy in his extension of welcome. As the years passed, Stephens' place was acknowledged even by Yeats, who could not be blind to the popularity of the Puckish writer whose place in the affections of the English reading public was securely established.

It would be impracticable to set down here every testimony relative to each individual's title to membership in the school. It suffices to have drawn together here representative statements wherein the terms "circle," "coterie," and "school" occur frequently enough to establish the fact that the attributions were actually those of the Irish writers themselves.

2. The Salon

The consciousness of themselves as a coterie is further attested by their development of another institution symptomatic of a school of writers, the *salon,* though the term connotes a greater formality than may rightfully be associated with the Irish. From the time of the beginning of the revival certain gathering places were recognized centers of literary life, and there both the poets and the critics assembled, and "for the most part the critics were the poets, and the poets were the critics."[23] In this way Stephen MacKenna made himself felt: "At MacKenna's evenings I would meet A. E., occasionally Arthur Griffith, occasionally John Eglinton, occasionally Arthur Lynch, in the early days John Synge who had been a comrade of Stephen's in Paris, Joseph Hone, Rudmore Brown, Osborn Bergin, Thomas Bodkin. The talk was the best that could be heard anywhere."[24]

George Moore prophesied well, though egotistically, of Coole as a sort of Minstrelburg:

Coole was beginning to be known to the general public at the time I went there to write "Diarmuid and Grania" with Yeats. Hyde had been to Coole, and had been inspired to write several short plays in Irish . . . . If Yeats had not begun "The Shadowy Waters" at Coole he had at least written several versions of it under Lady Gregory's roof tree. A. E. had painted in the park; now I was going there. "In years to come Coole will be historic; later still it will be legendary, a sort of Minstrelburg, the home of the Bell Branch Singers," I said.[25]

One could continue endlessly with references to A. E.'s Sunday evenings. Dunsany tells of meeting James Stephens in A. E.'s house in Rathgar Avenue, where "on Sunday evenings he always had a reception for such as cared to come, mostly poets."[26] At that time, Dunsany relates, James Stephens was excited by the approaching appearance of his first book, not yet quite believing that it should actually come to pass that he should see his book in a shop window.

Yeats refers to the "writers or would-be writers, among them James Stephens," who gathered at A. E.'s rooms regularly on Sunday evenings after A. E. had become a magnet because of his publication of *Homeward, Songs by the Way*. Yeats attended, but he confesses that he was "not friendly with that center, considering it made up for the most part of 'barren rascals'—critics as Balzac saw critics."[27]

3. The Irish National Literary Society

Consistent with the usual pattern of development in a school there developed out of the associations of these literary men the Irish National Literary Society, the National Theatre Society, which was to develop later into the Abbey Theatre, and the Irish Academy of Letters. Yeats defined the purpose of the Irish National Literary Society, founded in Dublin in 1893, referring at the same time to the Irish Literary Society founded two years earlier in London: "These societies had given, as I intended, opportunity to a new generation of critics and writers to denounce the propagandist verse and prose that had gone by the name of Irish literature, and to substitute for it certain neglected writers."[28]

Yeats recognized that they would have a hard fight before they would get the right of every man to see the world in his own way admitted. He said in a letter to John Quinn:

Irish national literature, though it has produced many fine ballads and many novels written in the objective spirit of a ballad, has never produced an artistic personality in the modern sense of the word. Tom Moore was simply an incarnate social ambition. And Clarence Mangan differed merely from the impersonal ballad writers in being miserable . . . . We will have a hard fight before we get the right of every man to see the world in his own way admitted. Synge is invaluable to us because he has that kind of intense narrow personality which necessarily raises the whole issue.[29]

Yeats' point of view was subscribed to wholeheartedly by Lady Gregory and A. E. and continues to be upheld by Daniel Corkery, an influential voice from southern Ireland. Corkery has said that the difference between Anglo-Irish literature and Irish literature is the difference between Maria Edgeworth's *Castle Rackrent* and Lennox Robinson's *The Big House,* that exploring one's own land for a foreigner is not expressing one's land for itself, and that much so-called Anglo-Irish literature might better be called Irish-English.[30]

Yeats and his followers were determined, obviously, to make of the new Irish literature a sincere expression of the Irish, an expression that would reflect the native culture and the character of the Irish stripped of all superimposed Anglican veneer. All pseudo-patriotism, all exaggerations such as had been perpetuated in the "stage-Irishman," all false wit, in short, all aspects of the literary lie were to be denied through the conscious agency of the Irish National Literary Society. In the application of the new spirit to the drama Yeats and A. E. were determined to go even further than they had in their treatment of the lyric and the short-story writer. The drama, the reformers felt, should stem from the heroic matter of the Gaelic legends.

Not all members of the group were in complete agreement with Yeats on this point. John Eglinton, better known by his pseudonym than by his real name, William Kirkpatrick Magee, a distinguished essayist, held divergent opinions regarding the Gaelic legends as adaptable subjects. A. E., while asserting his own faith in their continued power as symbols, records Eglinton's attitude:

> I know John Eglinton, one of our most thoughtful writers, our first cosmopolitan, thinks that 'these ancient legends refuse to be taken out of their old environment'. But I believe that the tales which have been preserved for a hundred generations in the heart of the people must have had their power, because they had in them a core of eternal truth . . . . These dreams, antiquities, traditions, once actual, living and historical, have passed from the world of sense into the world of memory and thought . . . . They have now the character of symbol, and as symbol, are more potent than history . . . . Deirdre is, like Helen, a symbol of eternal beauty, and Cuchulain represents as much as Prometheus the heroic spirit, the redeemer in man.[31]

Yeats was informed of Eglinton's view and made note of it as follows:

> Let a man turn his face to us, accepting the commercial disadvantages that would bring upon him, and talk of what is near to our hearts, Irish Kings and Irish legends and Irish Countrymen, and we would find it a joy to interpret him [on the stage]. Our one philosophical critic, Mr. John Eglinton, thinks we were very arbitrary, and yet I would not have us enlarge our practice. England and France almost alone among nations, have great works of literature which have taken their

subjects from foreign lands, and even in France and England this is more true in appearance than in reality.[32]

Stephen Gwynn, though not antagonistic, does not completely support the prevailing opinion and remains impenitent:

> The rest of us had not been taught as yet that it was unpatriotic to be amused by the songs which Robert Martin and Percy French were writing. I remain impenitent and think that what is called "Anglo-Irish" humour, when at its broadest, as in Robert Martin's *Ballyhooly* is very good fun indeed, and at its subtlest, as in Maria Edgworth or in much of Lever, or in the work which Robert Martin's sister, Martin Ross, did with Edith Somerville, is as good a humour as the modern world can show. As for its fidelity to life, no one who has lived in the west of Ireland, and, above all, no one who has taken part in Irish politics, is going to be convinced that the "stage Irishman" as Irish authors represented him is not a legitimate caricature. The truth has been that people took it for a complete representation.[33]

But these differences of opinion were but slightly felt and, in the main, one common purpose, the presentation of the real Ireland and the truly Irish, actuated the practice of the members of the Irish National Literary Society, whose dramatic expression led to the founding of the Abbey Theatre.

4. The Abbey Theatre

This is not the place wherein to recount the history of the Abbey Theatre, the facts of which are already too well known to demand notice here, but a few statements pertaining to the development of the theatre and the Academy are necessary at this point, however repetitious, to establish the base from which explorations depart into that morass of interlocking comment upon the persons engaged in these organizations. The comments selected are chosen to show again that common purpose which is requisite to any acknowledgment of the group as a school.

Lady Gregory confesses that the statement which was circulated in the form of a news letter at the time of the founding of the Irish Literary Theatre seems a little pompous. It begins:

We propose to have performed in Dublin, in the spring of every year certain Celtic and Irish plays, which, whatever be their degree of excellence, will be written with a high ambition, and so to build up a Celtic and Irish school of dramatic literature. We hope to find in Ireland an uncorrupted and imaginative audience trained to listen by its passion for oratory, and believe that our desire to bring upon the stage the deeper thoughts and emotions of Ireland will ensure for us a tolerant welcome, and that freedom to experiment which is not found in theatres of England, and without which no new movement in art or literature can succeed. We will show that Ireland is not the home of buffoonery and of easy sentiment, as it has been represented, but the home of an ancient idealism. We are confident of the support of all Irish people, who are weary of misrepresentation, in carrying out a work that is outside all the political questions that divide us.[34]

Yeats felt the necessity, even the urgency, of utilizing the national heritage for drama and roused in his contemporaries a sense of obligation toward their own people who had suffered from exploitation by writers in the old tradition. "All Irish writers," he wrote, "have to choose whether they will write as the upper classes have done, not to express but to exploit this country; or join the intellectual movement which has raised the cry that was heard in Russia in the seventies, the cry 'To the people'."[35]

Later, in the same work, he accents again the reference to class when he says: "Our opportunity in Ireland is not that our playwrights have more talent—it is possible that they have less than the workers in an old tradition—but that the necessity of putting a life that has not hitherto been dramatized into their plays excludes all these types which have had their origin in a different social order."[36]

But Yeats had no intention of sealing off the Irish dramatist in a provincial world of his own. He knew that a full knowledge of the history of the drama and its modern trends in other countries than his own was essential to the craftsman. With Martyn and the youthful Joyce, he recognized the master Ibsen:

It is of the first importance that those among us who want to write for the stage should study the dramatic masterpieces of the world . . . . At the present moment [1901], Shakespeare being the only great writer known to Irish writers has made them cast their work too much on the English model. . . . If Irish writers had studied the romantic plays of Ibsen, the one great master the modern stage has produced, they would not have sent the Irish Literary Theatre imitations of Boucicault, who had no relation to literature. . . . We Irish have, I think, far greater need of the severe discipline of French and Scandinavian drama than of Shakespeare's luxuriance.[37]

At the same time he felt that the impulse toward dramatic expression lay in the people themselves: '. . . we have turned a great deal of Irish imagination towards the stage. We could not have done this if our movement had not opened a way of expression for an impulse that was in the people themselves. The truth is that the Irish people are at that precise stage of their history when imagination, shaped by many stirring events, desires dramatic expression."[38]

Stephen Gwynn attributes to George Moore the calling of the Irish Literary Theatre to the attention of the English critics. Moore, he said, could never resist putting his finger into any new literary pie:[39]

Mr. Yeats understands to perfection the arts of the propagandist. This was quickened about March by the publication of . . . Mr. Edward Martyn's prose-drama, *The Heather Field,* accompanied by a preface from Mr. George Moore, who has throughout acted as sandwich man to the movement. Mr. Moore has the talent of awakening controversy, and though in describing Mr. Martyn's play as a masterpiece unique in modern prose-drama, he did Mr. Martyn a very ill turn, he certainly succeeded in calling the attention of English critics to the Irish literary Theatre and *The Heather Field* in particular.[40]

But Moore was apparently both a benign and an evil influence, in the opinion of Gwynn, who said that "the Irish Literary Theatre died either from inanition or a surfeit of George Moore."[41] Yeats, however, is generous in his acknowledgment of Moore's contribution: "Looking back now upon our work [The Irish Literary Theatre], I doubt if it could have been done at all without his [George Moore's] knowledge of the stage; and certainly if the performances of this present year [1901] bring our adventure to a successful close, a chief part of the credit will be his."[42]

Joseph Hone, Yeats' biographer, modifies this acknowledgment somewhat by calling attention to the fact that Yeats had "admitted that Moore was an embarrassing ally":

At this time [1897] neither Yeats nor Martyn had any working knowledge of the theatre, and Lady Gregory had never given a thought to the stage—was not even much of a theatre-goer. Yeats at once realized that Moore, who had always been knocking about theatres and had produced a play of his own in London, would be essential to their rehearsals. But several prominent characters of the Irish revival—George Russell among them—resented the introduction of Moore into the movement on the ground of his political as well as his religious shortcomings. Yeats admitted that Moore was an embarrassing ally ("he must always be condemning or worshipping") but found his "moral enthusiasm" inspiring.[43]

The loss of Synge, Colum suggests, rather than "a surfeit of George Moore" initiated the decline in this phase of the Irish literary movement. Colum sums up the accomplishment:

Synge died in 1909 and though his last play, *Deirdre of the Sorrows,* was still to be produced, and although many other important plays were afterwards put on, the date of Synge's death marks the end of a period of growth. We can now ask what the movement that created the Abbey Theatre has actually accomplished. Briefly stated, it has produced a national drama for Ireland: it has intensified in Irish writers national characteristics, and it has encouraged them to write plays that are charged with Irish temperament, the Irish instincts, the Irish tradition.[44]

A. E. Malone felt that the triumvirate, Yeats, Synge, and Lady Gregory, had no successors among the new dramatists of the Irish Theatre "where farce, melodrama, and cynicism now hold dominant sway."[45] This situation did not disturb Colum, who said, "After all, it is too much to ask of a country that she should look upon the production of literature as the be-all and end-all of the national life."[46]

5. The Academy

We have yet to consider the Academy as a tangible evidence of a conscious school of writers. George Moore, who "would have a finger in every pie," ignored the invitation to membership, and there were other refusals, as will be seen later. Perhaps Moore's dislike of Lady Gregory carried over finally to her last great project, for: "She [Lady Gregory] remained to the last by the side of Irish literature, and it was in her house that Yeats and George Russell discussed the project of an Academy of Letters which should carry on the tradition of their movement, make known the views of Irish authors on such questions as censorship and call attention to the respect due to the intellectual and poetical quality in the national life. Bernard Shaw consented to become President of the Academy, and George Russell drew up the rules and the constitution."[47]

Frank O'Connor, himself a member of the Academy, reflects the attitude of A. E. as an academician, an attitude not characteristic of that modest poet, as will be apparent later: "It [The Academy of Letters] was Yeats' idea, an institution whose authority might override mob law and fight the absurd censorship of books. A. E. was gloomy. He feared and distrusted those enthusiasms of Yeats and prophesied that the Academy would be asked to award a prize to some of Yeats' protégés.

. . . Once when I questioned the name of some suggested Academician, he said, 'Why worry about literary eminence? You and I will provide that.' "[48]

Hone indicates the more inclusive nature of the Academy as compared to that of the more limited theatre group:

The formation of the Academy was announced at a meeting in Dublin on September 18, 1932, when Lennox Robinson read out the letter, signed by Bernard Shaw and Yeats, which had been addressed to each of those invited to become members. The list was inclusive enough: The Celtic poets were there alongside the Cork Realists of 1910, Gaelic modernists like F. R. Higgins and Frank O'Connor, St. John Ervine and

21

Peadar O'Donnell, two Northerners, and Edith Somerville the "Big House" novelist. George Moore ignored the invitation and refusals on various grounds came from Douglas Hyde, Stephen MacKenna and James Joyce. Joyce's refusal was the chief disappointment. He . . . recalled that it was thirty years since Yeats had first held out to him a "helping hand" but added that his case being as it was and probably would be, he saw no reason why his name should have arisen at all in connection with such an Academy.[49]

6. The Decadence

The literary society, the theater, the academy were, indeed, both centers of and culminations of influences. John V. Kelleher in the *Atlantic* (March, 1945) pronounced the extinction of an Irish school of literature. He said that the death of F. R. Higgins, which had followed so closely the death of Yeats, had suddenly revealed the scarcity of poets in a country where poets had been as plentiful as journalists elsewhere. "Those who are left," he said, "do not coalesce into a school." He also noted the cessation of interlocking critical comments.[50]

St. John Ervine had said much earlier that the Irish Literary Renaissance had perished for lack of staying power,[51] setting down this opinion after the school had already demonstrated its vitality through thirty years of distinguished achievement. Today we can but acquiesce with the view of Kelleher, though Ervine's judgment proved to be hasty. A. E. protested a slightly earlier pronouncement: "A writer in the American *Dial* suggested lately [1923] that the Irish literary movement had come to an end, but the funeral oration he pronounced was premature. Since he wrote, Irish literature has been enriched by three notable books, *The Return of the Hero,* by Michael Ireland, the beautiful *Deirdre* by James Stephens, and lastly by the long expected novel of Padraic Colum, *Castle Conquer.*"[52]

Three years later Colum, expanding his *Bookman* article of July, 1926, acknowledged that the coterie had broken up, and he assigned a reason: "In the space between the downfall of Parnell and the rise of the Irish Volunteers the intellectuals had the whole stage in Ireland—I mean intellectuals in the best sense of that abused word. They formed a coterie that was homogeneous, in which everybody knew everybody's oddity . . . . They are still in Dublin, most of them; but the coterie has broken up; ideas have been de-limited, and have taken on a practical tinge because of the demands of the new state."[53]

James Stephens saw that the school had been absorbed into the world, that the culture of the Irish could no longer be considered as growing from its own root. He said, "We have entered the world. More, the world has entered us, and a double, an internal and external, evolution is our destiny."[54]

That the Irish literary revival was accompanied by the typical manifestations of a school—namely, a central coterie, a salon, a theatre, and an academy—is obvious, and, except for the less evident nature of the salon, was recognized by outsiders from the first. The whole activity was constantly under scrutiny and was being criticized by the participants themselves. The associates in the movement were conscious of themselves as playing a role and have left a record of a self-conscious expectancy of being acknowledged in literary history.

Chapter II

THE EXPATRIATE CONSIDERED

George Bernard Shaw, who had only occasional connections with the Dublin writers and who did not concern himself with analyzing their dispositions or powers, illumined a characteristic feature of the Irish in his play *John Bull's Other Island* when he had the Englishman Broadbent say to Boyle, "Here you are, belonging to a nation with the strongest patriotism! the most inveterate homing instinct in the world!"[1]

Practically all Irish writers felt the necessity for the Antaean touch of the soil of Ireland and they periodically gave expression to the longing for contact with the homeland. Joyce and Moore were notable exceptions. Joyce succeeded in completely divorcing himself in the flesh, though not altogether in spirit. His expatriation is foreshadowed in *A Portrait of the Artist as a Young Man,* wherein Stephen Dedalus, who is acknowledged to stand for Joyce in both the *Portrait* and *Ulysses,* said to himself that "his soul was disquieted and cast down by the dull phenomenon of Dublin."[2] Joyce, while still a young man, left Dublin, feeling a bitter disdain.

Eglinton tells us that Joyce was much disgusted by the scruples of the Dublin publishers who had destroyed the copies of Joyce's *Dubliners,* lacking the temerity to release what they had temporarily been willing to publish. According to Eglinton, Joyce had said, "I am going back to civilization," and Eglinton adds that that was the last he had seen of Joyce.[3] Frank O'Connor says that Joyce went away because he could not be bothered to stay at home and fight out elementary things.[4]

Although Joyce was able to quell this "homing instinct," he continued to find his subject matter in Irish life. However, by this very power of disassociation, which is so atypical, as will be seen when the attitudes of other members of the school are delineated, Joyce reached an objectivity which enabled him to see the universal implications in his Irish subject matter.

The Expatriate Considered

George Moore was well on his way toward being an expatriate when the voice of Ireland recalled him. It had been his belief that "an Irishman must fly from Ireland if he would be himself. Englishmen, Scotchmen, Jews," he said, "do well in Ireland—Irishmen never; even the patriot has to leave Ireland to get a hearing."[5] He did return, his convictions notwithstanding, and remained in Ireland for ten years, in a disgruntled state of mind for most of the period. He very soon complained to Yeats and Martyn, "It never does an Irishman any good to return to Ireland . . . and we know it."[6] When he was forced to admit that his hopes for reviving Gaelic were fruitless, and when he had convinced himself that no Catholic people could ever produce a culture, he sought someone on whom to fasten blame for his return to Ireland, and his fancy alighted at various times on Yeats, A. E., Edward Martyn, the English, and even Cathleen ni Houlihan.

Moore said, variously, in *Hail and Farewell,* that he might never have gone to Ireland if he had not met Yeats,[7] that it was A. E. who had brought him to Ireland, knowing that Ireland needed his help,[8] that his rewriting of Martyn's *Tale of a Town* had reawakened the Irish that was lying dormant in him, and that "a voice" heard on three different occasions had bidden him pack his portmanteau and return to Ireland.[9] Reflecting upon the Boer War, he had previously declared that "England had become so beastly" that he had had to come away. "The lust for blood," he said, "was in everybody's face."[10] And, more singularly, he blamed Cathleen ni Houlihan for his failure to remain apart from Ireland: "I began to tremble lest the terrible Cathleen ni Houlihan might overtake me. She had come out of that arid plain, out of the mist, to tempt me, to soothe me into forgetfulness that it is the plain duty of every Irishman to disassociate himself from all memories of Ireland—Ireland being a fatal disease, fatal to Englishmen and doubly fatal to Irishmen."[11]

Not all Irish expatriates had Moore's practical reason for leaving Ireland. As the date for the publication of *Ave,* the first book of his trilogy, *Hail and Farewell,* approached, he reflected that it would be in bad taste to remain on the scene:

"He [Heinemann, publisher of *Ave*] had written, 'Are you coming to live in England?' meaning nothing very probably thereby, but setting me thinking all the same that it would be in bad taste for me to remain in Dublin meeting my friends and acquaintances in the street, my models, and when the letter slipped from my hand to the floor I foresaw how exile would give the book a definite distinction."[12]

One can never be sure of the actual feeling of the mercurial George Moore. Yeats once said that he and Moore would both get along better with the public if he himself could keep from saying everything he believed and if Moore could keep from saying what he did not believe.[13] Whether or not George Moore really felt that Ireland was "a fatal disease," or whether he was merely talking for effect, the subject matter of the book upon which his reputation largely rests derived from his yielding to the "homing instinct" for a decade.

Other members of the school were certain of the necessity for contact with Ireland. A. E. wrote to Stephen MacKenna: "I am sure you will find Ireland is your spiritual home and come back to it. I never pretended to be anything specially national but I would be in despair if I had to live outside Ireland."[14]

He had written earlier:

Ireland is now self-governing. The passion which held many of its exiles to it, and made them think of themselves as Irish even to the third generation born out of Ireland, must be dissipated unless we can create so intense an intellectual life here that the needles of their being will be turned to it as to a spiritual or cultural home, as Islam for long looked to Mecca, or Jewry to Jerusalem. . . . If all the famous living Irish writers had their homes in Dublin it would perhaps be the most brilliant centre of poetry, drama and story in the world.[15]

A. E.'s dream of Dublin as an intellectual center kept him watchful of straying talent. He reasoned with Frank O'Connor, who was thinking of leaving Ireland, saying, in effect, that Ireland would excite him creatively by her opposition to his ideologies. The fact that Ireland was "pious and hide-bound" was, said A. E., the very situation that stimulated intellectual revolt and intellectual self-consciousness among the Irish writers who were Pagans or free-thinkers. "Take care," said A. E., "lest in choosing a nation of free-thinkers you do not destroy the diversity between the world without and the world within which makes you a writer."[16]

A. E. expressed a personal horror of the occasional duty visit to the Irish Literary Society of London: "I find that when I go over there, my soul absolutely won't go with me, and I am merely a body walking about while my soul is in retreat in some old mountain in Ireland. . . . I dare say I might get accustomed to it . . . but my soul might get tired waiting here for me and I might reincarnate in another body and my state when I returned be worse than before."[17]

Yeats, likewise, according to Joseph Hone, "was not a flower that could flourish on foreign soil," and it was Hone's belief that "Oxford or any other place outside Ireland could only be a diversion for him, however long he might stay in it. His inspiration ultimately depended upon the roots he had formed in Ireland, and he expressed the hope and belief that the end of his life would be as full of Irish activities as the start of it."[18]

L. A. G. Strong speaks movingly of Yeats' homesickness in exile: "London never won Yeats's affections, and he and his sister lamented fiercely, beside the drinking fountain at Holland Park, their exile from the home of their grandparents, longing for a sod of Sligo turf to hold in their hands."[19]

Yeats, himself, in a letter to Katherine Tynan, expressed a horror of London akin to that felt by A. E.: "London is always horrible to me. The fact that I can study some things I like here better than elsewhere is the only redeeming fact. The mere presence of more cultivated people too is a gain, of course, but nothing in the world can make amends for the loss of green field and mountain slope, and for the tranquil hours of one's own countryside."[20]

The professional journalist-editor Stephen Gwynn felt much as did Yeats and A. E. Although Gwynn, who was born and grew up in Ireland, earned his living for the most part in

England, he never let a year pass without spending at least a month in his own country. "It would be unfair," he said, "to take what I have to say, as it has sometimes been taken by Irish critics, for the remarks of a mere casual visitor."[21]

Darrell Figgis noted that it was part of the paradoxical nature of Synge that, though he wandered in Europe, he could be at home only in Ireland.[22]

John Eglinton, who has lived in England since the "Treaty" of 1921, long before his self-imposed exile was thinking soberly on the subject of the cosmopolitanism of the Irish and compared them to the great men of the Middle Ages, who, as a rule, distinguished themselves in another country than that of their birth. The gifted sons of Ireland, he acknowledged, had, as a rule, never forgotten that they were Irish.[23] Much later he gave a detailed explanation of his feeling for Ireland as a country as an emotion contrary to his feeling for Ireland as a nation. Although he disliked "the green flags and reedy orchestrations of nationalist demonstrations" he felt that no Irishman could with entire impunity "relinquish all the associations of childhood and youth with delectable places."[24]

The Irish writers, in the main, felt a warm attachment to their native land and readily admitted that a complete emancipation was impossible. Just what they thought Ireland to be, and just what representations of her they believed to be faithful delineations, will be subject to review in the following chapter.

Chapter III

THE IRISH MIND AND CHARACTER

Both the expatriate and the nonmigratory Irishman spent a great deal of thought on the analysis of their countrymen's habits of mind and action, often with the purpose, as previously suggested, of estimating an author's genuineness and his sincerity of expression. A. E. once said that "it would be a fascinating theme for intellectual criticism to review the Irish character as manifested in Irish literature from its earliest apparition [sic] in the sagas down through the centuries, its modifications by the invasions until we come to its contemporary manifestations."[1] Informal and sporadic attempts to do this sort of thing can be traced in the critical comment of the modern Irish school.

Although Yeats said in his *Autobiography* that "one cannot sum up a nation intellectually, and when the summing up is made by half-educated men the idea fills one with alarm,"[2] he, nevertheless, has contributed much general and specific comment on the character of the genuine Irishman. Sometimes his opinion of Paudeen is not flattering, and he denounces him as unable to do more than fumble in his greasy till.[3] At times he takes a more poetic view of him:

I am certain that the water, the water of the seas and of lakes and of mist and rain, has all but made the Irish after its image. Images form themselves in our minds perpetually as if they were reflected in some pool. We gave ourselves up in old times to mythology, and saw the gods everywhere. We talked to them face to face, and the stories of that communion are so many that I think they outnumber all the like stories of the rest of Europe. Even today our country people speak with the dead and with some who perhaps have never died as we understand death and even our educated people pass without great difficulty into the condition of quiet that is the condition of vision. We can make our minds so like still water that beings gather about us that they may see, it may be, their own images, and so live for a moment with a clearer, perhaps even with a fiercer life because of our quiet.[4]

29

The foregoing appreciation was set down in the most idealistic period of Yeats' youth. Six years later in his preface to *The Unicorn from the Stars* he struck a contradictory note, deploring the poor taste of the Irish in the arts and their hatred of personal reverie, the habit of personal reverie being the very characteristic for which he had previously commended the Irish.[5]

The poet's idea of Ireland, Yeats insisted, must be examined critically. If it were found to be based upon artificialities built up by commonplace men or tinged with false emotionalism disguised as patriotism, its influences, he thought, would be deleterious in proportion to the degree of falsity of the idea. By this criterion he approved Allingham and Ferguson, whose love of Ireland he felt was based on a genuine emotion for a definite locale, and cast out Davis, whose poetry, he said, derived from a superficial jingoism. Yeats regretted the artificial idea behind the poetry of Davis because he felt it had done him harm. "I tried to free myself from it," he said, "and all my enemies come from my fighting it in others."[6]

Yeats' approbation of Synge rested largely on the fact that his "grotesque plays" held "so much of the mind of Ireland." The plays of Synge revealed, he said, "the unbroken character of Irish genius."[7] He felt that Synge was produced by Ireland through the very force of contrariety in mood as an expression of the secret soul of Ireland:

When a country produces a man of genius he never is what it wants or believes it wants; he is always unlike the idea of itself. In the eighteenth century Scotland believed itself religious, moral and gloomy, and its national poet, Burns, came not to speak of these things but to speak of lust and drink and drunken gaiety. Ireland, since the Young Irelanders, has given itself up to apologetics. Every impression of life became at last impossible, all was apologetics. There was no longer an impartial imagination, delighting in whatever is naturally exciting. Synge was the rushing up of the buried fire, an explosion of all that had been denied or refused, a furious impartiality, an indifferent turbulent sorrow. His work, like that of Burns, was to say all the people did not want to have said. He was able to do this because Nature had made him incapable of a political idea.[8]

Yeats measured James Joyce against the real Ireland and found in him "our Irish cruelty, also our kind of strength" and compared his "cruel, playful mind" to that of a "great soft tiger cat."[9] Yeats, who usually insisted on the mystic and poetical fancy of the Irish, acknowledged even the more un-palatable matter in Joyce to be genuinely derived from the authentic Irish tradition. He agreed with Joyce himself, who, in the person of Stephen Dedalus, had said, "This race and this country and this life produced me . . . . I shall express myself as I am."[10]

Yeats frequently praised Lady Gregory for her greater knowledge of the country mind. Her plays reflected her ab-sorption in the folk-mind of Ireland, he said. She had found her matter in the folk-tale and had discovered the cadence of the peasant dialect. Adding to these her personal style or artifice, she had reflected "the glory of the world in a peasant mirror."[11]

These views seem realistic enough. But Maud Gonne, who until political interests completely diverted her was asso-ciated with the school, tells us that Yeats' own notion of Ire-land was wholly "idealistic." "To Willie," she said, "less aware of the people than of the Land, Ireland was the beauty of unattainable perfection, and he had to strive to express that beauty so that all should worship."[12]

A. E. Malone feels that Yeats has wholly misinterpreted the Irish mind and character. He cites *Beltaine*,[13] wherein Yeats had said that the intellect of Ireland is romantic and spiritual rather than scientific and logical. Malone says that the Irish intellect is really exact and logical and that the Irish intellect pushes logic to such extremes that it is mistaken for romance. He even goes so far as to explain the comparative unpopularity of Yeats' plays in Ireland as due to his seriously misjudging the Irish character. "He has given to the world," writes Malone, "a false interpretation of that character by en-dowing it with his own ideas and beliefs."[14]

Yeats was attacked by the Irish press at the time of the formation of the Irish Academy of Letters on the ground that it was not in accord with true Irish nationality. Its membership, which was drawn up in large measure at the direction of Yeats, was said to be "alien to true Irish ideals."[15] Clearly, Yeats' notion of what constituted the genuine Celtic sometimes met with opposition.

In his study Yeats possibly felt that Holy Ireland was, as he said of Kathleen, daughter of Houlihan, "purer than a tall candle before the Holy Rood,"[16] but in the Senate[17] he more often remembered Paudeen fumbling in his greasy till. In his creative practice Yeats was motivated by an illusion, an idealistic conception of his country, by an Ireland of the imagination, but in his critical estimates of his countrymen and of contemporary literary craftsmen he was able to think realistically. While considering Yeats' ability to measure the Celtic element it would be well for one to bear in mind what he wrote in *Samhain*: "It is always necessary to affirm and reaffirm that nationality is in the things that escape analysis. We discover it, as we do the quality of saltness or sweetness, by the taste, and literature is a cultivation of taste."[18]

A. E., who said that "a nation exists primarily because of its own imagination of itself,"[19] felt that a national literature was obligated to find the ideal national mind and to reveal it:

Every Irishman forms some vague ideal of his country, born from his reading of history, or from contemporary politics, or from an imaginative intuition and this Ireland in the mind it is, not the actual Ireland, which kindles his enthusiasm. For this he works and makes sacrifices; but because it has never had any philosophical definition, or a supremely beautiful statement in literature which gathered all aspirations about it, the ideal remains vague. This passionate love cannot explain itself; it cannot make another understand its devotion. To reveal Ireland in clear and beautiful light, to create the Ireland in the heart, is the province of a national literature.[20]

The Celtic poets, A. E. contended, had always had the faculty of abstracting from the land which they beheld another Ireland which was the Ireland of the visionary eye. This inner Ireland was the reality for A. E., who could not think of it as other than "the shadow of the thought of God."[21] He called this power of idealizing, the "psychic dominant" of the

Irish mind and the prevailing feature of Irish poetry which sets it apart as unmistakably racial in quality.

Outside influences were, A. E. believed, incapable of obliterating this hallmark of Irish fancy and imagination. The Irish writer is no less Irish in essence, he said, because he happens to receive outside influences, than was Shakespeare other than English because he grafted on to his own genius ideas from the Renaissance. A. E. acknowledged that Liam O'Flaherty had learned from the Russians, George Moore from the French, W. B. Yeats from the French symbolist poets and the Japanese Noh-plays, and Edward Martyn from Ibsen. But the impact of world ideas and forms had no more been capable of disintegrating the national soul of the Irish than had Hellenic, Roman, and Renaissance sources been effective in disrupting the organic unity of Shakespeare, of Milton, of Shelley, or of Keats.[22]

A. E. frequently judged his associates in the light of the source of their inspiration. James Stephens, Austin Clarke, and Synge were still, he said to R. C. Feld in 1921, the greatest names in modern Irish verse because they "stood robed in the colors of an ancient Ireland which was once again coming into the glory that had been hers." James Stephens had failed at first, he said, because he had been "aping and imitating" the English. "He was not himself and he was not Ireland." When finally he had turned "humbly and reverently" to the "deep and many-colored waters of Gaelic legend" he had risen "renewed in spirit and rejuvenated in power." Now that Stephens was no longer a disciple of false gods, but "a prophet of gods that were true," A. E. declared him to be creating literature that would live.[23]

While A. E. was assessing the Celtic features of his fellows, he was, of course, being evaluated in his turn by this criterion. Lord Dunsany, who had said near the beginning of *My Ireland* that the typical Irishman would not be met within his pages, chiefly because there was no such thing, attempted, nevertheless, to get at the characteristic features of the Irish and to apply them to the poets. He said of A. E.: "He was so Irish in his poetry and in his love of the hills and streams of Ireland, and even in his Oriental air, that we may hope that some men something like him may one of these days be found in Ireland again."[24]

Dunsany made much of this Orientalism as being a characteristic feature of the Irish mind. He recalled an Irish legend that claimed for certain districts in County Cork a population descended from the peoples of Barbary. "One can see clearly enough," he wrote, "in the minds of the Irish people a certain lore, a wise way of looking at things" which "seems to come from the East and which shows now and then in their talk, like flashes of gold that has come from a far country."[25] He quotes Kipling as having said, "By every test that I know, the Irish are Oriental."[26]

St. John Irvine regarded A. E. in a different light, criticizing his fellow Ulsterman for his taint of Irish sentimentality: "Sometimes I say to myself that A. E. has lived too long and too exclusively in Ireland. He is not free from the mush of sentimentality with which Irishmen regard themselves."[27]

George Moore, shortly after he had returned to Ireland, said to a young friend that he noticed Ireland was spoken of "not as a geographical, but a sort of human entity."[28] While taking stock of this "human entity" Moore deplored the fact that Ireland was tainted through and through with peasantry. "True," he said, "that every family begins with the peasant; it rises when it rises through its own genius. The cross is the worst stock of all, the pure decadent."[29] This view of the Catholic peasant as decadent is ironically out of harmony with the Celtic reformers' tendency to exalt the peasantry. Elsewhere Moore commended P. T. Gill's *Express* as "the first paper that had attempted to realize that Ireland had an aesthetic spirit of her own."[30]

Moore likewise pondered over the Celtic strain in his contemporaries and thought that there was "more race" in Yeats than in anyone he had seen for a long while.[31] He considered Douglas Hyde particularly Celtic in appearance: "He spoke with his head thrust over his thin chest as they do in Connemare. Yet what name more English than Hyde? It must have come to him from some English ancestor—far back indeed, for it would require many generations of intermarriage with Celtic women to produce so Celtic an appearance."[32]

While Moore was considering the Irish qualities of his associates, he was in turn being judged. A. E.'s secretary, Susan Mitchell, a member of the coterie and one of the few women who frequented the gatherings of the literati of Dublin, would classify him as Irish, though it obviously pained her to do so:

In "Parnell and his Ireland" I find proof of Mr. Moore's nationality as an Irishman, because the contempt and scorn in it are too bitter to be the work of an alien. The gibe that we fling at an alien glances off because our knowledge of him is seldom intimate enough to point it, but when we desire to wound our own people, knowing the vulnerable spots, our shafts get home. There is to me more indecency in "Parnell and his Ireland" than there is in those of Mr. Moore's books where this characteristic is said to predominate. It is indecent in the revolting display he makes of his country's hurt.[33]

Furthermore, Miss Mitchell, in her study of George Moore, probed deeply the question, "What is an Irishman?" She said that everyone who wrote about Ireland took it for granted that Ireland was a sick country, and that each writer had his nostrum. But opinion was divided, she said, over the identity of the patient. She felt that the Irish were too busy being Catholics, Protestants, Unionists, and Nationalists to betray any national character. But George Moore, she contended, had given his Irish character a chance to emerge by resisting "the temptation common to every Irishman to obliterate himself in a movement."[34]

John Eglinton, speaking of Moore's *A Story Teller's Holiday,* said that for the first time Moore was by virtue of that book "as much an Irishman as ever was Yeats in *The Celtic Twilight.*"[35] He associated the "good-humored indecency of Moore" with the "more malign irony of James Joyce" as indicating a movement in the direction of change in the Irish mind.[36]

Eglinton defined at length the typically Irish, but he made a subtle distinction between the "Modern Irishman" and the "Mere Irishman": "A less invidious name for the Anglo-Irishman would now perhaps be the Modern Irishman, the Irishman, namely, who accepts as a good European the connection with Great Britain and yet feels himself to be far more distinct from the Anglo-Saxon than he is from the Mere Irishman."[37]

He spoke of "the pretense, which imparts an almost Della Cruscan artificiality to the Irish Literary Movement, that the Mere Irishman is the Modern Irishman." He defined the typical Irish writers as those who live by their imagination rather than by their intellect, and he commented shrewdly on the incapacity for doubting as an Irish trait:

Perhaps the Celt is right in regarding doubt as an intellectual limit beyond which he dares not, or does not care to, tread. It must be said, however, that the habit of subordinating intellect to imagination has brought the Celt neither blessedness nor greatness. His visionary disposition is partial to that conservatism which has so greatly helped his enemies. So long as the other world lies within call and prospect, there will never be any active instinct to redress the wrongs of this. Had the Celt ever permitted himself to doubt, had he called in the aid of reason, his history would have been different.[38]

In a spirit of mockery, or in a tone of light banter, Oliver St. John Gogarty in *Going Native* considers the two Irelands, the one a geographical concept, and the other a state of mind. As he contemplated leaving Ireland, he felt that he was really getting out of a state of mind. "I have to remove myself," he said, "from the vacuous, the dreamy, the perpetually inept life."[39]

In an earlier work Gogarty suggests that the character of St. Patrick was modeled upon the character of the Irish, and he elaborates upon the analogy between the Saint and his people:

There is no saint in any country who is so familiar to the inhabitants, and I may say, using it in a secondary sense, with whom the people are so familiar. What does St. George mean to the Prime Minister of England? An heraldic figure on an obsolete coin. And St. David is not much of an inspiration or a comfort to the miner of Wales. It is not about him they joke. He is dated and dead. But with St. Patrick it is different.

He is not dead. He is everyone's familiar . . . .

Therefore it is interesting to work back and to inquire how far the character of the Saint can be deduced from the character of his people. It is the same thing if we inquire how far the Irish people have taken after the Saint.

What are the characteristics of the Irishman? Primarily he is a sportsman and an agriculturalist. He is quick to anger. . . . He is a lover of Song in a Land of Song. His physical energy is prodigious, and he is capable of asceticism, as the numbers of our monks witness. He is full of ardour and proud nobility . . . .

Now these traits might be the traits of the Saint himself. He was given to fishing and gardening—a Roman accomplishment. He was impatient in his zeal. But the identity of the Saint and his people needs no better proof than the many thousands who are called by that patrician name of his.[40]

Gogarty notes the innate love of natural scenery among the Irish and dwells upon Ireland's pre-eminence as a land of song. He deplores the lack of the will to action. "We have too much soul and we lack sang-froid. We lack the power to accomplish," he wrote.[41]

James Stephens looked critically for that Irish singing quality in Gogarty's verse. Stephens differentiated English poetry from Irish in this, that the former sings in the line and the latter in the word. By this criterion he judged Gogarty's verse and concluded, "His poetry is not breathed in the Irish manner . . . . The Celt in Dr. Gogarty is already promising that if he can forget his scholarship he will . . . sing like a lark instead of like a musician."[42]

The minor poet-critics were sometimes hard on the Irish. L. A. G. Strong thought the Irishman hard to work for. "He has a habit of denying patriotism to all who do not think as he does."[43] This opinionated manner did not make for smooth relationships. He felt that "the Irish people, with their graphic violence of speech, their wild humour and their poetic exaggerations made magnificent material" for Yeats. Moreover, he felt that Yeats could have been produced in no other country than Ireland.[44]

Katharine Tynan contrasted the Irish and the English aphoristically: "The Englishman likes to sit still and have his mind improved. The Irish want to improve other people's minds." She made it clear that the Anglo-Irishman is neither English nor Irish: "The Anglo-Irishman, although he achieves great things at times, is, in the rank and file of him, somewhat harsh. He has the John Bullish attitude towards sentimentality without the real sentiment which John Bull is unaware of possessing, although it jumps to the eye of everyone else. He has somewhat of the Celt's irritability and jealousy; in fact, these things grafted upon him make for an intolerance which is far from being Celtic."[45] She said of herself that she had the "self-consciousness and suspicion of the Celt in contra-distinction to the Anglo-Saxon effusiveness and confidence in its kind."[46]

Although Yeats had made a great point of Lady Gregory's understanding of the people, A. E. Malone said that she never penetrated their minds. He granted that she could reproduce the peasant speech, but he maintained that she saw the people from without. Malone implies that her "unconscious snobbery" precluded her understanding the people or being understood by them. Her characters, he said, "have none of that shrewd cunning which is the mark of the peasant in Ireland as elsewhere."[47] He did grant, however, that *The Workhouse Ward* was representative and that *The Canavans* satirized the Irishman's determination to be on the winning side at any cost, with a faithful presentation of that trait.

Edward Martyn, likewise, was not sufficiently Irish, according to Malone. He was too fastidious, too literary, too European.[48] St. John Ervine, on the other hand, "exposed and examined" all the ills of Ireland. In his *John Ferguson* was "embodied all for which Ulster stands, . . . all that makes Ulster fascinating."[49] Stephen Gwynn also said that Ervine's work was "an excellent expression of the Ulster mind."[50] Doubtless there are those who would disclaim the Ulster mind itself as typically Irish and would discount these preferential opinions accordingly.

Stephen Gwynn once said that in looking for distinctive characteristics of a literature one must acknowledge that no literature can be reduced to a formula. But he felt that the

Irish were "peculiarly sensible to the beauty of vagueness, of large, dim, and wavering shapes."[51] In his application of this criterion he remarked that although Dr. Hyde wrote in Gaelic for Gaels, he was actually less Celtic than were Yeats and other writers in English.

It is apparent that the members of the modern Irish school were at all times conscious of their race. There was a constant interplay of comment relative to the genuineness of the representation being made of the Irish by the Irish, and this comment rested upon an initial consideration of just what basic characteristics constitute the Irish mind. The members of the school did not agree as to what habits of mind predominated, nor was the individual critic at all times consistent in his own point of view. In these few references brought together here the critics have called the Irish visionary, imaginative, meditative, grotesque, cruel, strong, romantic, spiritual, exact, logical, Oriental, sentimental, decadent, indecent, ironic, vacuous, dreamy, inept, irritable, jealous, self-conscious, and suspicious. The interest lies, in this study, not so much in the agreement or disagreement of the various pronouncements as in the observation of the fact that the method of criticism employed by the critics of the modern Irish school followed a constant rather than a variable pattern. The critic scrutinized the Irish mind and character for the purpose of establishing criteria by which he subsequently estimated the worth of all who purported to make a literary representation of the Irish.

Chapter IV

THE ATTITUDE TOWARD THE ENGLISH

The attitude toward the English is one facet of the Irish mind. There is scarcely an Irish writer, either of the modern Irish or the Mere Irish, as Eglinton so ingeniously divides them, who has not been expressive in this regard. The modern Irish writers weighed each other's prejudices, and their opinions are but slightly diversified. As literary leaders of Ireland they show a surprising loyalty to the English, for the most part. This anomalous fact is scarcely taken into account by those who condemn the Irish for their separatist movement.

The members of the Irish school were with few exceptions members of the Nationalist party, abjuring the Unionist treaty so long as it refused to give Ireland unfettered control over taxation and trade policies, and yet denouncing the radical militaristic Sinn-Feiners, or Republicans, as they were later to be called. The Nationalist took a middle position between the Unionist, who was usually a descendant of the English and whose habits and traditions were more English than Irish, and the Sinn-Feiner, who claimed descent from the more ancient Celt and whose distaste for the merest echo of English custom called for the complete repudiation of that culture.

Yeats was so strong a Nationalist as to be excluded from the ruling society during his youth, particularly during the period of his close association with the militant agitator, Maud Gonne. He remained a Nationalist to the end, but his attitude toward England became warmer as he reached maturity. George Moore gives us a picture of him in his early years speaking against Dublin's Trinity College, which was tantamount to speaking against England:

Yeats rose, and a beautiful commanding figure he seemed at the end of the table . . . . He drew himself up and spoke against Trinity College saying that it had always taught the ideas of the stranger, and that was why Ireland had never listened and Trinity College had been a sterile influence. The influences that had moved Ireland deeply were the old influences that had come down from generation to generation, handed on by the story tellers that collected in the evenings around the fire, creating for learned and unlearned a communion of heroes.[1]

Speaking of him in his maturity, Joseph Hone says that "when Lady Gerald Wellesley reproached him for encouraging 'hate between nations' he replied that he was shocked by her thought. 'How could I hate England, owing what I do to Shakespeare, Blake, Morris? England is the only country I cannot hate.' "[2]

In his *Autobiography* Yeats frequently expressed regret for the cultivation of Anglophobia in Ireland. He manifested his disapproval of that bitterness in his commentary on *The King of the Great Clock Tower,* and he detailed conditions of political confusion in Ireland which were to deflect the attention of the Irish and relieve England for a time from being the object of political hatred. The new dispute, commonly referred to as "The Parnell Split," effected this transfer of animosity:

Dublin had once been a well-mannered, smooth-spoken city . . . . Then came agrarian passion; Unionists and Nationalists ceased to meet, but each lived behind his party wall an amiable life. This new dispute broke through all walls; there are old men and women I avoid because they have kept that day's bitter tongue. Upon the other hand we began to value truth . . . free discussion appeared among us for the first time, bringing the passion for reality, the satiric genius that informs *Ulysses, The Playboy of the Western World, The Informer, The Puritan,* and other books, and plays; the accumulated hatred of years was suddenly transferred from England to Ireland. James Joyce has no doubt described something remembered from his youth in that dinner table scene in *A Portrait of the Artist as a Young Man,* when after a violent quarrel about Parnell and the priests, the host sobs, his head upon the table, 'My dead king.'

We had passed through an initiation like that of the Tibetan ascetic, who staggers half dead from a trance, where

41

he has seen himself eaten alive and has not yet learnt that the eater was himself.[3]

As did Yeats, A. E. grew melancholy when he contemplated the excesses of the Republicans. He wrote to Yeats in May of 1932, "Dublin is depressing these days. Ireland seems . . . like a lout I knew in boyhood who had become a hero and then subsided into a lout again. The events of the last twenty-five years have brought no age into the thought of the people."[4] At the same time he was writing to Kingsley Porter, "I fancy that after some months of independence the majority will want to be back in the British Commonwealth, and I am not sure the Briton will want us back."[5] Earlier that year he had written to Porter that De Valera's policy terrified him and he confessed that he did not like his party or its ideals. The reason he gave for his dislike was ingenuous, and quite in character. He observed that there was not a poet among De Valera's followers and that the party did not inspire poetry. "A cause that has no poets," he said, "is doomed to perish."[6] This is quite a departure from an earlier attitude expressed in a letter to Stephen MacKenna, his politically radical friend, in 1924, when de declared himself to be an anarchist in his soul.[7]

Moore puts A. E. on record as a supporter of Home Rule, the status favored by the Nationalists: " 'Home Rule,' said A. E., 'will set free a flood of intelligence.'

" 'And perhaps the parish priest will drown in this flood [Moore's remark].'

"A. E. did not think this necessary."[8]

Frank O'Connor says of A. E. that "he was not a success in London, and he hated England and the English."[9] A. E. was not an extremist. He was devoted to Ireland first and last, but he had no desire that Ireland should dissolve every political connection with England. He decried the complete domination of Westminster, but would have preferred Home Rule, or dominion status, to complete separation.

Synge was, according to Yeats, incapable of thinking a political thought. "With the exception of one sentence, spoken when I first met him in Paris, that implied some sort of nationalist conviction, I cannot remember that he spoke of politics or showed any interest in men in the mass," wrote Yeats.[10] Samuel Synge, the brother of John Millington, in a letter to his daughter, quoted Lady Gregory as having said of J. M. Synge that "he seemed to look on politics and reforms with a sort of tolerant indifference." Samuel Synge, reflecting upon this, said that his brother did not quite know what to do with Ireland. "He wished to see her people better and happier, but he did not feel very sure how these conditions were to be brought about."[11]

Stephen MacKenna in a letter to Arthur Lynch, in the autumn of 1928, presents Synge as being far from passive in his objection to certain expressions of the Nationalist spirit. MacKenna said that Synge gently hated the Republican, Maud Gonne, and loathed the Gaelic League. Synge himself knew Irish, had even won a prize at Trinity College, Dublin, for proficiency in the language. He was furious over the dissemination by the Nationalists of the pamphlet lie that to learn Modern Irish would give the learner access to the grand old saga literature. MacKenna writes that he had never forgotten the bale in Synge's eyes when he said, "That's a bloody lie; long after they know Modern Irish, which they'll never know, they'll still be miles and years from any power over the saga."[12]

Martyn was one of the most extreme Nationalists within the Irish literary school. As a young man he had been a Unionist, Denis Gwynn tells us. But he had "hated Gladstonian Liberalism as English demagogy." His interest in the national revival in letters made him increasingly anti-English, and finally the influence of the historian, Lecky, made him an extreme Nationalist, though Lecky himself was a Unionist.[13]

Lady Gregory records George Moore's bewilderment over the position he found himself in after praising Martyn's *Maeve* profusely. That play had come to be interpreted as strongly Nationalist in spirit. Moore had not yet come out openly for Home Rule. Martyn probably wrote with allegorical intent, but the play was mild in comparison with certain of his hysterical pamphlets which, according to Denis Gwynn, attacked the "vulgarity and hypocrisy" of the English. Martyn went so far as to declare that the worst features of the Irish character and taste had been derived from the English. He deplored the emulation of England by the upper classes in Ireland, for the reason that they had eschewed every good thing England had to offer and had embraced only her coarsest materialism.

Martyn was at least consistent in his ardor, but George Moore wavered in his moods and was troubled by his confused feelings for England: "In the dusk England seemed to rise up before me in person, a shameful and vulgar materialism from which I turned with horror, and this passionate revolt against England was aggravated by memories of my former love of England, and, do what I would, I could not forget that I had always met in England a warm heart, a beautiful imagination, firmness and quiet purpose."[14] At times he spoke contemptuously of the English, as when he said that he fell out with his friend for appearing so arrogantly English in his dress, or as when he recorded his disgust with the sheeplike faces of the English.[15]

Denis Gwynn would have it that Moore's antipathies toward the English were roused by Martyn, who had become rabidly anti-English at the time of the Boer War. However that may be, it is doubtful whether George Moore ever felt more antagonistic toward the English than he did toward the Irish. He certainly felt more contempt for Catholic Ireland than he ever felt for Protestant London. Certainly his *Bending of the Bough* was a dramatic satire on Irish politicians. Lady Gregory said that it was "the first play dealing with a vital Irish question that had appeared in Ireland." She remarked upon the impartiality of its thrusts: "No one is really offended, certainly not the Nationalists and we have not heard that the Unionists are either."[16]

According to A. E. Malone, Lady Gregory herself was especially strong in political satire. "The majority of her plays are capable of political interpretation," he said, and added that her work "might almost be read as a continuous commentary upon the Irish political scene during her lifetime."[17]

Lady Gregory dated "the setting free of the imagination of Ireland" with the death of Parnell.[18] Vitally interested in the Land League, wholly conversant with the peasant and his needs, Lady Gregory consistently championed the Irish cause. But this did not awaken in her any irreverence for the cultural past or present of the English. She never indulged in any bitter recriminations or denunciations of the English or of their supporters in the Unionist party in Ireland.

John Eglinton noticed that the Anglo-Irish fostered the Irish dislike of the English, a dislike that was "curiously combined with a preference for the society of the English people."[19] He said, further, that the belief in a "Holy Ireland" had always given "a kind of religious fervour to Irish patriotism," and that as long as he could remember, it has been mixed up with the belief that "materialistic England" was "tottering to its fall."[20] Without, of course, sharing personally in the animosity, he felt that hatred of England was the very support of modern Irish literature: "Hatred of England is, in fact, the keystone of modern Irish literature; it is a 'value' in Irish thought too important and too 'structural' to leave out. The term, however, is a vague one, denoting the whole system of things which has deprived the Modern Irishman no less than the Mere Irishman of his destiny."[21] Eglinton himself is clearly on the side of England: "To this race destiny entrusted the task of unifying and governing Ireland as clearly as to the Anglo-Norman race it committed the task of unifying and governing England; and towards the end of the eighteenth century we seemed in a fair way to fulfill our trust. But when the premature introduction of democratic ideas into Ireland at the time of the French Revolution led to a completely artificial political situation in which the country's natural rulers had to look on while England made what bargain she could with the subject race, the Modern Irishman [Anglo-Irish] lost interest to a great extent in his own country."[22]

Lord Dunsany tried to dissipate the Irish animosity toward

England by jocular comment. No doubt he hoped that the restless Irish might read his implication with salutary results. He questioned the Irish as follows: "We owe to England a sum of about five million pounds on account of certain Land annuities . . . . But to whom shall we pay the debt? To the English? Certainly not. What are they, only a lot of Angles, Jutes, Saxons and Danes, and Normans? and what right had any of them—that's what we want to know—what right had they to come to England at all?"[23]

It seems clear that the Irish writers who have the most enduring reputations were conscious of their debt to English and European culture and, while never condoning injustice in the English, were equally unwilling to condone a bitter hatred of the English evident among certain classes of Irish society. Perhaps the viewpoint has never been more cleverly put than by Francis Hackett in his introductory note to Gogarty's *As I Was Going down Sackville Street:*

> Imagine a Catholic Irishman called Gogarty who is christened Oliver St. John. The Oliver escorts him to Dublin Castle to the Tories, while Gogarty clings to the Quays. Gogarty goes to Cecilia Street to the Catholic Medical School, and Oliver "cleared out of that place in three weeks." Gogarty worshipped Griffith and saw Collins plain, while Oliver genuflects to Austen Chamberlain . . . .
>
> Too Gogarty to be a Die-Hard, too Oliver to be a Separatist, he was born betwixt and between, yet it is this very dissatisfaction that sharpens his wit and brightens his eye.[24]

The members of the literary school were sympathetic with all movements toward the betterment of domestic conditions for the Irish, actively urged a re-emphasis upon the Irish heritage of Gaelic culture, and leaned heavily toward, if not actively avowing, the Nationalist party principles. Aware of the dangers of armed Republicanism, they questioned their own ardor, and when the dark days of rebellion came they stood aghast at what their propaganda for literary nationalism had seemingly aided and abetted. Stephen Gwynn had gone home from the performance of *Cathleen ni Houlihan* asking himself whether such plays should be produced "unless one was prepared for people to shoot and be shot,"[25] and when those premonitions were fulfilled, Yeats suffered agony of heart and gave voice to his dejection in the poem, "Easter 1916," each stanza of which concludes with the refrain, "A terrible beauty is born."

In *Going Native* Gogarty gives us a vivid picture of Yeats as an aging and disillusioned man:

His sorrow arose not from the trivialities of a trivial people. It came from a deeper source: Why had the Irish people raised their hands and ruined all that stood for culture and comeliness in the land? Why, to put it in his own words, were the lesser streets turned upon the great? Why were the mansions of the country with their statues and pictures and silver-smiths' art, mansions which belonged to men with better Irish blood and more reckonable names than the commonality, why were these destroyed? He was wondering had any of his poems incited the peasants to revolt and to turn on beauty . . . .

I assured him thoughtlessly that it was not so. And yet . . . he was betrayed by the very terms of the imagination with which he had endowed his countrymen . . . .

Suddenly he turned on his chair, afire with vehement speech. "Ouseley, you must go! You must leave this country! You cannot go on filled with bitterness or chilled with contempt for the little office-seekers and rude civil servants which is all that Ireland, left to itself, has made of its freedom. The Anglo-Irish are the salt of the earth. They are being persecuted. You must fly with the wild geese. You must go. To stand still is to sink in the bog."[26]

Perhaps the poet-critics would all basically have preferred with Yeats "the pure joy that only comes out of things that have never been indentured to any cause."[27] Of one thing we may be certain: few, if any, of the modern Irish writers remaining in 1938 from the Dublin literary coterie took any pleasure in the final triumphs of De Valera and his party. And, finally, one must say that it appears paradoxical that the pacific and Protestant[28] Douglas Hyde, who strove so hard to keep the Gaelic League out of political channels, should have become the first president of Eire largely by the vote of Catholic Republicans.[29]

Chapter V
THE LANGUAGE PROBLEM

The developments within the Gaelic League[1] and the militant activity of the Irish Volunteers[2] were reciprocal to no small degree. Douglas Hyde in his *Literary History of Ireland,* published in London in 1899, stressed the five-century struggle between the Irish and English which had culminated in the forced imposition of English on the schools of Ireland, where schoolmasters who knew no Irish were attempting to teach children who knew no English. English, though reinforced by statute, might not have dominated completely had it not been for the Famine[3] which had depopulated precisely those districts wherein lay the last strongholds of the Gaelic. Now that the very existence of the language was endangered, Hyde, imbued solely with educational and moral enthusiasms, began actively to propagandize for the preservation of a culture by the revival of the language which was the garment of that culture. In an article entitled "What Ireland Is Asking For," which first appeared in the *All Ireland Review* of November 3, 1900, and which was reprinted later in *Ideals of Ireland,*[4] he summarized the situation: "With broken English came the laying waste of the mind of a people who were as quick in speech, as quick in business, as able, as witty as any people in the whole of Europe, but who were left as blind, as dull, and as dark as any wild untaught natives."[5]

Quite different was the spirit of Arthur Griffith, whose interest in Gaelic was motivated primarily by his purpose to de-Anglicize the Celt. He wished to raise the language as a bulwark against the political suzerainty of England. The two streams of activity were to merge as Dr. Hyde's scholarly impulse broadened into a movement to save not merely the traditional language and literature, but also the music and dances and sports of the Irish peasant. The enlargement of aim drew more and more supporters into the movement and captured the popular imagination. The Gaelic League, the organized center of the activity, spread rapidly throughout

Ireland, and throughout Great Britain and the United States as well. The many units of the organization offered convenient centers for political fomentation.

Stephen Gwynn tells us that the League was "non-political and non-sectarian" and that "Hyde spared no effort to keep it so."[6] Denis Gwynn says that Hyde's resignation from the presidency of the League was a gesture of protest made "when he could no longer prevent it from becoming a political body."[7] Nevertheless, the persistent propaganda of the Irish Volunteers, emanating from those radical in outlook, led finally to the identification of the Volunteer movement and the work of the League. This fusion of the Volunteers and the League was recognized by Padraic Colum when he wrote: "Neither the Gaelic movement alone nor the Volunteer movement alone could have created the racial pride, could have brought about the challenge to a power that seemed securely entrenched in Ireland—it took both together to make the temper that was behind such a challenge."[8] In spite of the political implications of all this diversified activity of the Gaelic League, there were enrolled in its membership many whose primary interest lay in the revival of Gaelic as a medium of literary and social expression.

The members of the modern Irish literary school were naturally involved in the revival of the Gaelic language. Although they were soon known as leaders of that aspect of the movement that had to do with the revival of the themes of the Celtic saga and the employment of folk dialects in their own verse and drama, their attitudes on the question of the re-establishment of the racial tongue have scarcely been noted. Yet each member of the school took a definite stand on the question of language predominance. Each made frequent assertions relative to his own attitude, and from time to time alluded to the stand his associates had taken.

Douglas Hyde is generally credited with being the founder of the Gaelic League. Thus it comes about that Stephen Gwynn attributes the modern Irish revolution to the Divinity School of Trinity College, "for a theological student Hyde was, though he never passed into orders: and the Gaelic

League came from Hyde, and from the Gaelic League came the movement that was called Sinn Féin."[9] Trinity College would feel no gratification over being called, even so indirectly, the seed plot of the Republican movement, but that is by the way.[10]

Likewise recognizing Hyde's leadership, Yeats, in *Dramatis Personae,* says that Hyde's lecture, called "The De-Anglicisation of Ireland," delivered at the National Literary Society on the occasion of his becoming its president upon the retirement of John O'Leary, led to the foundation of the Gaelic League.[11] The story is a familiar one and is supported by many references. But slight exceptions have been taken, and other claims have been presented. Denis Gwynn says that Hyde was not in fact the real originator of the language revival, for the first arrangements had already been made by Professor Eoin MacNeill, who organized "a small class for teaching Irish to a few enthusiasts in Dublin."[12] Stephen Gwynn also gives credit to MacNeill, saying that he had taken as much part as Hyde had in the founding of the League, but that he had "lacked altogether Hyde's extraordinary power to advance its growth by personal appeal."[13] According to Katharine Tynan, the League originated in London under the supervision of a Mrs. Roe and a Miss Thompson: "Mrs. Roe was a grand-daughter of John Foster, the last Speaker of the Irish House of Commons, and she and her sister, Miss Skeffington Thompson, were ardent Irish patriots. At that time they were watching over and tending a little society at Southwark which had begun to teach the London Irish children Irish history, Irish poems, Irish songs and dances—the seed of the Irish Literary Society, and of a bigger growth, The Gaelic League."[14]

By raising the question of origins these remarks serve eventually to reinforce Hyde's position as one who fostered the League. There is actually little disagreement with Joseph Hone, who wrote: "Gradually it became apparent that Hyde was to create a popular movement, far more important in its practical results than any movement Yeats could have made, and that the Gaelic League would conform to moral and educational enthusiasms alien alike to the folk spirit and to the aristocratic and critical Nationalism which Yeats had learned at the feet of John O'Leary."[15] Not only did Lady Gregory write appreciatively of Hyde as the founder of the League, but she also made plain the connection between the language movement and the theatre development: "It was a movement for keeping the Irish language a spoken one, with, as a chief end, the preserving of our nationality. This does not sound like the beginning of a revolution, yet it was one. It was the discovery, the disclosure of the old folk-learning, the folk-poetry, the folk-tradition. Our theatre was caught into that current, and it is that current, as I believe, that has brought it on its triumphant way."[16]

George Moore, who, for a number of years, was one of the most ardent supporters of the language movement, said that "an analogy exists between Douglas Hyde's position towards the English language and Dante's and Milton's position towards the Latin language."[17] Such a statement is a further reminder that the Dublin school were self-consciously motivating the Renaissance of Irish letters. Had not all literary revivals had their language problems? Further analogies were drawn. For example, Stephen Gwynn argued that if the Provençal tongue were worth reviving, then the Irish was much more so, since it was "the richest in records of the old Celtic tongues, any one of which has a continuous history going back for many ages before the dialects of Latin took shape."[18] Various supporters of the revival called attention to the success of the Welsh, who, in a like venture, had brought the number speaking that language up from ten thousand to nine times that figure. The critics cited revivals of Flemish and Bohemian a quarter of a century earlier. They reminded their readers that all over Europe a desire to preserve the languages of small and weak nations was asserting itself.[19]

The most concerted effort to publicize the movement was that made by A. E., D. P. Moran, George Moore, Douglas Hyde, Standish O'Grady, and W. B. Yeats, who, under the editorship of Lady Gregory, reprinted certain of their arguments, which had appeared in current magazines, in book form as *Ideals in Ireland.* Of this group Moore was the most vocal in the first decade of the new century, making public addresses here and there, and contributing to periodicals highly emotionalized tracts in favor of the revival of Gaelic. All this ardor did not activate him to learn the Irish language, however. It was easier to implore others to master the tongue. In fact, Yeats accuses Moore of laziness in this regard: "He did not want to go to Mass because his flesh was unwilling, as it was a year later when the teacher, engaged to teach him Gaelic, was told that he was out."[20]

There has been disagreement as to whether Moore was genuinely interested in the movement or was merely enjoying a pose. Susan Mitchell takes a curious attitude in calling his interest a "sincere pose." Her analysis runs: "We Irish are very much aware of ourselves as actors. We seldom lose ourselves in it, but Mr. Moore's dramatic concern with himself is so much inwoven in his nature that he can only be really himself in the various poses he assumes. He is absolutely sincere in each, and his Gaelic pose had for him a momentous importance that provoked the merriment of Dublin."[21]

On the other hand, John Eglinton said that Moore was genuinely interested in the Gaelic movement and that he "fussed and worried Hyde" with suggestions for translating foreign masterpieces into Irish.[22] Moore himself declared that he was proud to have had some of his stories, which were later published in English as *The Untilled Field,* translated into Irish to serve as models for young Irish writers of the future. He said that his stories, when translated back from the Irish into English, had gained by their bath in Gaelic. He likened them to "a jaded townsman refreshed by a dip in the primal sea."[23] He also made note of how his interest in Gaelic had been aroused. It was the conversation between himself and Martyn when the two were living in London garrets in the Temple in 1894 which started him thinking about Gaelic, he said. Martyn had said that he wished he knew enough to write his plays in Irish. Moore exclaimed: " 'You'd like to write your plays in Irish! . . . I thought nobody did anything in Irish except bring turf from the bog and say prayers.' "[24]

There follows the record of Moore's thoughts on the subject: "'So Ireland is awakening at last out of the great sleep of Catholicism!' and I walked about the King's Bench Walk, thinking what a wonderful thing it would be to write a book in a new language or in the old language revived and sharpened to literary usage for the first time."[25]

Thus it came about that Moore "took not only the literary theatre but the Irish language under his wing,"[26] according to Stephen Gwynn, who said further that "Moore's convictions were always passionate while they lasted."[27] Indeed Moore sometimes waxed maudlin: "And a vision rose up before me of argosies floating up the Liffey, laden with merchandise from all the ports of Phoenicia, and poets singing in all the bowers of Merrion Square and all in a new language that the poets had learned, the English language having been discovered by them, as it had been discovered by me, to be a declining language, a language that was losing its verbs."[28]

There is no doubt that Moore for a time threw himself energetically into propaganda for Gaelic, furnishing articles to periodicals in which he declared that it was primitive peoples who invented languages and journalists who destroyed them,[29] in which he likened the Gaelic language to a handful of wheat in an Egyptian mummy case,[30] reminded his readers that Ibsen wrote a language spoken by only a few million people, but had an audience in the whole of Europe, and said that Homer's audience was no larger than Douglas Hyde's.[31] In his "Plea for the Soul of the Irish People" Moore declared: "In five years it has become an honor to know the language which in my youth was considered a disgrace."[32] In this same article, which was profuse and lengthy, Moore said that there was something inexpressibly shocking in the destruction of a language. He felt that such a destruction was "an act of iconoclasm more terrible than the bombardment of the Parthenon or the burning of Persepolis." And, finally, he reminded the English that what they were giving the Irish in exchange for their lost inheritance of heroic legends and epic cycles was merely the refuse of "the gutter press of London."[33]

Was Moore in earnest? By his own confession his argu-

ments were "merely intellectual, invented so that the Gaelic
League should be able to justify its existence with reasonable
literary argument."[34] He contrasted his own attitude with that
of Yeats, whose feelings in the matter were, Moore said, of
his deepest nature. Moore has, furthermore, left us an uncomplimentary picture of Hyde speaking Gaelic, a vignette which
shows a surprising scorn for the language on which he had
elsewhere been expending sentimental and exhortatory encomiums. Thus the protean Moore:

> His [Hyde's] volubility was as extreme as a peasant's come
> to ask for a reduction of rent. It was interrupted, however, by
> Edward calling on him to speak in Irish, and then a torrent
> of dark, muddied stuff flowed from him, much like the porter
> which used to come up from Carnacun to be drunk by the
> peasants on midsummer nights . . . . It seemed to be a language
> suitable for the celebration of antique Celtic rites, but too
> remote for modern use. It had never been spoken by ladies in
> silken gowns with fans in their hands or by gentlemen going
> out to kill each other with engraved rapiers or pistols. Men
> had merely cudgeled each other, yelling strange oaths the
> while in Irish, and I remembered it in the mouths of the old
> fellows dressed in breeches and worsted stockings, swallowtail
> coats and tall hats full of dirty bank-notes, which they used
> to give my father. Since those days I had not heard Irish, and
> when Hyde began to speak it an instinctive repulsion rose up
> in me, quelled with difficulty, for I was already a Gaelic
> Leader.[35]

Although Edward Martyn was irritated by Hyde's efforts
to keep the League out of politics, he never withdrew his support, and gave tangible evidence of his faith in its purpose by
leaving a legacy to endow the training of Irish-speaking teachers. Along with his friend Moore, he contributed articles to
the newspapers from time to time in support of the revival of
Irish, but, unlike Moore, he had the fortitude to acquire a
reading knowledge of its modern form. Although he disliked
committee work of all kinds, he served faithfully for years as
a member of the executive committee of the League.[36] Denis
Gwynn, who eulogizes Martyn for this, as well as for other
services performed for other phases of the cultural resurgence,
notes that he also caused the movement "considerable em-

barrassment" by bringing George Moore in as an "ardent recruit."[37]

But was George Moore the recruit of Edward Martyn? John Eglinton says that Yeats, who was not so deeply interested in the revival of the Irish language as Moore had believed him to be, had capitalized on Moore's enthusiasm for Gaelic and had imported Moore for the purpose of "discomfiting the bigwigs of Anglo-Irish culture like Dowden and Mahaffy."[38]

Regardless of who may have been instrumental in bringing Moore into the movement—and it is not unlikely that mere curiosity and desire to be in the thick of any Irish agitation at the moment would have drawn him to Dublin without any personal pressure—it is evident that Moore's opinions veered from one point of view to another without any consistent underlying logic. But whatever changes of attitude Yeats reflected were the result of a natural development from the enthusiasm of youth to the conservatism of maturity.

As early as October, 1906, in an article, "Literature and the Living Voice," in *The Contemporary Review,* Yeats told of going to the village of Killeenan to do honor to the memory of Raftery, the Gaelic poet, as the villagers gathered to erect a headstone over his grave. He noted the difference in appearance between the people of Killeenan and those of Galway only twenty miles to the north. "A few miles," he said, "had divided the sixteenth century with its equality of culture, of good taste, from the twentieth, where if a man has fine taste he has either been born to leisure and opportunity or has in him an energy that is genius."[39] This experience helped him to interpret the language movement:

> It is some comparison like this that I have made which has been the origin, as I think, of most attempts to revive some old language in which the general business of the world is no longer transacted. The Provençal movement, the Welsh, the Czech, have all, I think, been attempting, when we examine them to the heart, to restore what is called a more picturesque way of life . . . . That this is the nobler element in the attempt to revive and preserve the Irish language, I am very certain. A language enthusiast does not put it that way

to himself; he says, rather, "If I can make the people talk Irish again they will "be the less English"; but if you talk to him till you have hunted the words into their burrow you will find that the word "Ireland" means to him a form of life delightful to his imagination, and that the word "England" suggested to him a cold, joyless, irreligious and ugly life.[40]

This attitude shows Yeats' sense of the practical. He recognized the inadequacy of Gaelic as a medium for transacting the general business of the world. Moreover, he felt that a distinctively national literature could be written in English. His interest lay in disseminating the native literature in translation and in drawing upon native literature for subject matter in creating the new literature. He wished to see the old Irish manuscripts preserved and published, to see all the dialects recorded, and he would not discourage the popular study of Gaelic or of modern Irish, though he had not learned the language himself. But he had no feeling that Irish was any longer the mother tongue of the Irish people. In the Senate he denounced the trend toward the imposition of Gaelic as a "piece of make-believe that would tend to bring Gaelic into contempt with honest minds."[41] Yeats understood enough of the history of language development to know that language change comes slowly and imperceptibly. The effect of forced change, he feared, would be "a long barren epoch" as far as literary productivity was concerned.

Writing of "Nationality and Imperialism," A. E. proclaimed some support of the movement, showing the usual antipathy toward Trinity College: "A blockhead of a professor drawn from the intellectual obscurity of Trinity, and appointed as commissioner to train the national mind according to British ideas, meets us with an ultimatum: 'I will always discourage the speaking of Gaelic wherever I can.' We feel poignantly it is not merely Gaelic which is being suppressed, but the spiritual life of our race."[42]

Eventually A. E. grew suspicious of the movement because it had "a pack cry."[43] He considered seriously and with practicality the questions: "What life would there be for a man of genius writing in Gaelic? . . . Is it likely men of genius will give up the hope all genius has of imparting its own imagination to myriads?"[44] He cautioned his readers not to conclude that he was opposed to Gaelic. He was, he said, "only filled with a spirit of reasonable scientific inquiry," which "made him poke his pen into a nest of wild bees not to destroy the bees but to see what would happen."[45]

George Moore had discussed the matter with A. E. and has left a record of their differing attitudes: "We fell to talking of the Irish language, I maintaining that it would be necessary to revive it, A. E. thinking that the Anglo-Irish idiom would be sufficient for literature."[46]

Moore based his doubts of A. E.'s visions on the fact that A. E. did not know the Irish language. Surely the old Celtic gods would scarcely deign to appear to one who not only did not know Irish, but did not even believe in the usefulness of the language.[47]

A. E. said to R. C. Feld, who has recorded his statement, that he did not think the poets would write in Gaelic, because they did not need to. He said that the spirit, the form, and the inspiration could be Celtic without its necessarily following that the language should likewise be Celtic. He mentioned James Stephens. His poetry, he said, although English, was in sound and rhythm Gaelic.[48] In an issue of *The Survey* devoted exclusively to the new government and to studies of the social conditions in Ireland, issued shortly after the 1921 treaty, A. E. wrote: "I feel assured, whether or not a modern literature in Gaelic be created, the characterless culture imposed on young Ireland in the national schools will be superseded, that the Irish people in a generation or two of free development will have a civilization as distinct in character as the Japanese."[49]

A. E., then, it is evident, was in agreement with Yeats. Neither man wished to curb any philological interests developing in the awakened Ireland, but neither felt that the poet should hamper himself by the restraints of a tongue now become foreign to him. Both men believed that English had by the slow process of time become the mother tongue of the

Irish and that the remnant of those speaking Irish were hardly the spiritual leaders of the present race.

Synge and Lady Gregory were of nearly the same opinion, although both knew Gaelic and could speak with and understand the peasants of the West. Their knowledge was fruitful for Irish literature. But they never entertained any notion that Gaelic should be restored to the drawing room or the market place, and certainly their own creative interest lay in the use of the Anglo-Irish dialects rather than in the employment of Irish. Synge's attitude was so well advertised as to bring him into disfavor with the Gaelic League and the Sinn Feiners, who soon constituted the larger part of the League's membership. Concerning this Stephen MacKenna wrote to A. E.: "They tell me, and I see many signs of it, that to value Synge's work is to be dreaded and disliked by the entire Gaelic League."[50]

MacKenna was one of those who regretted the loss of Irish. He wrote to Edmund Curtis in 1924, "Irish like Ireland is doomed; there is one God and Progress is his Prophet."[51] Colum tells us in his preface to MacKenna's journal that Mac-Kenna's house was the headquarters of a branch of the Gaelic League. Affairs were discussed in Gaelic. If one were at a loss for a Gaelic word, he might use a French or a German one, but English was under taboo.[52]

MacKenna's interest was deep-seated and sincere. He took great pains to learn the language and he raged against those who considered Irish as a patois for peasants. He expressed regret that he had learned the language too late to be able to make it the medium of his own literary expression.[53] What MacKenna could do with a language acquired by the painful process of self-tutoring is one of the triumphs of translation.[54] Colum says that MacKenna deplored the perfunctory interest taken by Yeats in the language revival, for he felt that the movement was expressive of the whole of Irish nationalism and that he made his intimates "ashamed that they had any other interests except the language one."[55]

Colum may have caught his enthusiasm for Gaelic from MacKenna. He wrote hopefully of Gaelic as a modern literary medium as late as 1924, when he said, accompanying his remark with a slight modification, that he felt sure there would be a modern literature in Gaelic. His reservation ran: "However, I think that the writer who will produce great work in Gaelic will have to remake the language; he will have to fuse the Munster and the Connacht idioms; he will have to accept and use boldly the Englishisms that have come in; he will have to draw from Middle Irish and perhaps from Scots Gaelic."[56]

Stoutly opposed to this optimistic support by Colum were the views of John Eglinton, who said that the ancient Irish language was "no more a bond of union among the Irish than Hebrew has been among the modern Jews."[57] In June, 1922, shortly after Irish political triumphs had emphasized the problem anew, Eglinton wrote in his Dublin letter for *The Dial*: ". . . Ireland can no more go back to Gaelic than England after Chaucer could go back to French or Anglo-Saxon."[58] Whereas Martyn and MacKenna had likened the beauties and fine nuances of the Gaelic to the Greek, Eglinton told Moore that the Irish language struck him "as one that had never been to school."[59]

In an early discussion of the movement, Eglinton had said that it was rather by a "thought movement" than by a "language movement" that Ireland would have "to show that it holds the germs of true nationality."[60] In a vein of cool logic, he denounced the plan of dividing Ireland into two camps, or two rival populations like the Jews and the Samaritans. He reminded Gaelic enthusiasts that "it was among the lost sheep of the house of Israel—amongst those who had lost the use of the Hebrew language—that the Jewish Messiah appeared."[61] He preferred that the Irish would speak in a human rather than in a national capacity. In fact, the term "Irish language" is "only a title of courtesy," he said. "The ancient language of the Celt is no longer the language of Irish nationality. In fact it never was," he wrote in his preface to *Bards and Saints*.[62]

Eglinton has given us a priceless description of "The Grand

Old Tongue" through the symbol of the Irish peasant. He wrote not unsympathetically:

> To us who are condemned to tread the pavements of a large and sophisticated town, his presence wafts an agreeable pungency of peat-smoke, the airs of boglands under the moon, the mists and eternal cadences of the Atlantic. Notwithstanding the homely burr in his accent, and a certain suggestion of a lack of book-learning and culture conveyed by his manner of slurring his syllables and running his words into one another, the general impression of dignity made during the slightest intercourse with him is such that no one dreams of raising concerning him the question whether he is a gentleman. And, indeed, when we reflect that his ancestry can be traced as far back as that of any of his compeers of Europe and Asia, the question would seem sufficiently superfluous.

After speaking of the great difficulty of learning to know "The Grand Old Tongue," he continued:

> . . . his talk is of turf-cutting on the mountainside, the kettle on the hob, the green boreen, or twilight trysting places . . . . Several learned doctors have pronounced that he cannot live much longer . . . . His admirers . . . scout this verdict . . . . It is very doubtful, however, whether those who indulge these fancies are the best friends of the old gentleman, whose infirmities and peculiarities are more suited to a life of retirement and rusticity. Those intellectually desperate men, who would hurry him into an impossible position as champion of political and religious parties, misconceive entirely the true nature of his mission, and, as might be expected, such persons are for the most part ignorant of the old man personally. It is, at all events, permissible to hope that under the care of the good friends whom he has found in his decline, he may live on now without much losing ground for an indefinite number of years . . . . For his presence sheds an old-world distinction over the whole island which was once his own, and to every hill and stream of which he bestowed in the morning of his youth a name.[63]

"The Grand Old Tongue" had no appeal for James Joyce. The first version of *A Portrait of the Artist as a Young Man* makes explicit the slightness of his contact with the Gaelic League. The fragment, edited from the manuscript in the Harvard College Library and published as *Stephen Hero,* devotes a few pages to argument upon the subject of the Irish language revival. Stephen [Joyce] confesses that his attendance upon a Dublin branch of the League was solely for the purpose of developing his acquaintance with a young lady who had attracted him. This "dark, full-figured girl"[64] is given the fictitious name of Miss Clery.

Stephen's views are not, however, voiced for Miss Clery, but are presented in conversation with his friend Madden. They may be summarized as follows: The Roman rather than the English tyranny had overborne the Irish intelligence; the Irish language was encouraged by the priests to preserve the Irish people from the Protestant "wolves of disbelief";[65] the enthusiasts did not care what banalities were expressed so long as they were expressed in Irish; the Irish peasant and his language represented no very admirable type of culture and all this fervor was the manifestation of false sentiment.

Stephen began a course of lessons in Irish. "He bought the O'Growney's primers published by the Gaelic League, but refused either to pay a subscription to the League or to wear a badge in his buttonhole. He had found out what he had desired, namely, the class in which Miss Clery was."[66] But Stephen's contempt for the methods and objects pursued by the League soon made him drop the connection in spite of Miss Clery's charms.

Padraic Colum calls attention to the comic overtones in Joyce's burlesqued elementary Gaelic lesson in *Ulysses*: ". . . 'Will you have a drink, Citizen?' says Joe to the Cyclops. 'I will, honorable person,' is the reply, and the pseudo-Gaelicism of a literal translation of a first lesson in Irish has a humor that only those who knew the town at the time would be aware of."[67]

Stephen Dedalus' knowledge of Irish was said by Joyce to be "theoretical" and "confined to certain grammatical rules of accidence and syntax and practically excluding vocabulary."[68] Joyce never learned Irish, though he was eminently distinguished for his wide proficiency in languages. He presents Gogarty, the Buck Mulligan of *Ulysses*, as contemptuous of the tongue.[69]

Gogarty, on his own part, has his joke at the expense of the revivalists. In *Going Native* he sets down his observation with his characteristic wit:

Captain Olley's Airways are as good as, if not better than, most of the air services of the world. It is not his fault that the little Irish company which took toll of him should have painted a name in Irish on the wing: *Aer Lingus.* Of course there is no word for Airways in Irish, there never was; but that is no reason why the attempt to make a name should make a mistake. The word *lingus* occurs only in Latin as a part of a medical term of which the less said the better. But even the English machine had to suffer from the fatuity of the country and the foolery of the patriots whose patriotism largely consists in an attempt to revive an old language by turning it into an unintelligible new.[70]

The Ulsterman, St. John Ervine, with his usual acerbity speaks of "the ancient Gaelic literature of which we hear so much and see so little."[71] With a somewhat irrelevant interest in the Russians he declared that they were dying of disease and hunger "with less complaint than a Sinn Feiner makes about his obsolete language which he cannot speak, will not write, and does not wish to learn."[72]

Investigation shows that the modern Irish school of writers did not go along with those governmental agencies which have made a knowledge of modern Irish requisite to civil service appointment and which have decreed that the Irish language be included in the curriculum of all national schools of the twenty-six counties of Eire.[73] George Moore's erratic enthusiasm was soon dissipated. Edward Martyn died before the fulfillment of his nationalist hope, but died leaving a legacy for the support of the program, and may, therefore, be considered exceptional. Yeats and A. E. did not confuse the issues in their enthusiasm for a revival of Gaelic culture. Synge and Lady Gregory, as well as Yeats and A. E., looked upon English as the mother tongue of the modern Irish. John Eglinton and Joyce were clearly opposed to the imposition of the Irish language on an Anglo-Irish people, and indulged in mockery of the movement, mockery which was even more pronounced in the caustic wit of Gogarty and the spirited jibes of St. John Ervine.

Yeats, A. E., Moore, and Joyce never troubled to learn either Gaelic or modern Irish, Martyn had only a fair knowledge of modern Irish, and the same may be said for Eglinton. Synge and Lady Gregory, as is well known, were proficient in both Gaelic and modern Irish, the latter distinguishing herself by her translations of the old sagas of Ireland's heroic age. Both Synge and Lady Gregory knew that a people trained to speak and read modern Irish would be no whit the more capable of reading Gaelic literature in the original. The popular conception of language values was rooted in ignorance. The educated coterie of the Dublin school did not join in with the "pack cry," as A. E. called it, and such confusions as have resulted in Eire since the processes of law have intervened cannot be attributed to the leadership of Ireland's men of letters.

Chapter VI

SOME LITERARY COMPARISONS, CHIEFLY EXAGGERATED

Although the Irish critic made a fairly thorough analysis of the Irish character, he overlooked at least one tendency that shows itself in the critical essays of the Dublin school. The Irish writers, at least, whatever one may say for the general public, took themselves very seriously. A sober self-aggrandizement, tinged with a naïveté which precludes any annoyance on the part of the reader, exhibits itself in the exalted comparisons drawn with the typical Irish precipitancy. The group, who were actually writing a history of the Irish Literary Society within a few months of its first meeting, were also comparing themselves to the Greeks, to Dante, to Shakespeare, to Goethe, and to other masters from the time of the first stirrings of literary activity. Standish O'Grady had announced in his weekly *Review* that Slievenamon would yet be more famous than Olympus.[1]

That Yeats seriously compared Synge to Aeschylus can scarcely be doubted, since the occasion of the comparison is on record from the pens of several commentators who, in this instance, seem to have perceived the humor of a more than slightly exaggerated estimate. George Moore would not, of course, overlook the opportunity of making Yeats appear absurd and records anecdotally: "When Synge came up from the country to read 'Riders to the Sea' to the company, Yeats, who did not wish to have any misunderstanding on the subject, cried 'Sophocles' across the table, and fearing that he was not impressive enough, he said: 'No, Aeschylus.' "[2]

Colum would have us believe that the comparison became a current joke among Dubliners and that it actually had a deleterious effect upon Synge's reception in Dublin:

There was nothing about Synge to make a crowd throw up a hat for; he was a made man in a city of men in the making; he could not have been a popular figure in Dublin. But his work might have been presented in such a way that it would have been tolerated from the beginning and that it would have been respected before his own end. And this would have happened, I believe, if the entrance for him had not been made somewhat intimidatingly. "A play that is like one of Aeschylus's," William Butler Yeats announced when he had read "Riders to the Sea." "Who is Aeschylus?" "Oh, he's the man who writes like John Synge." In that characteristic way Dublin countered the claim that Yeats set up.[3]

Later Gogarty recounts the incident, adding the liveliness of comic dialogue:

One of the first meetings of the Irish Theatre, or rather of those who were about to produce Irish drama, took place in the Nassau Hotel. Maud Gonne sat on the opposite side of the table. Synge was at one end by Lady Gregory. Patrick Colum sat next to me. Suddenly Yeats exclaimed in admiration of a scene he was reading:
"Aeschylus!"
"Who does he mean?" Colum whispered, amazed.
"Synge who is like Aeschylus."
"But who is Aeschylus?"
"The man who is like Synge!"[4]

But Mary Colum would not have the tribute to Synge taken lightly and insists upon its justice:

The young undergraduates of Dublin, reading the Greek dramatists for examination, used to smile with the brilliant ignorance and condescension of youth when Yeats would compare Synge to the Greeks, for the artists had to fight against the academic mind as well as against the national propagandists. But, to anyone reading these plays at this date [December, 1935] side by side with the Greek dramatists, the resemblance is there inescapably. It is in *Deirdre of the Sorrows,* in *Riders to the Sea,* even in *The Playboy.* There are the same strong, easily recognizable emotions, shaped, molded into types. Synge's is the very type of carefully wrought art in a dawning literature.[5]

Yeats went further than impromptu comment and is more explicit in print, pointing out that the thought of Synge's peasants "when not merely practical, is as full of traditional wisdom and extravagant pictures as that of some Aeschylean chorus, and no matter what the topic is, it is as though the present were held at arm's length."[6]

Gogarty, who laughed at Yeats for calling Synge the Dublin Aeschylus, in emphasizing A. E.'s power of communicating his own spirit says that in this respect he is like Plato, the artist who brought to his followers a realization of their own divinity and intensified it. Like Plato he taught nothing, Gogarty said, but he communicated himself, "and the best in himself, which consists of poetry, loving kindness and a passion for beauty more than for anything else."[7] Gogarty was writing seriously at this point and not, as he often does, with tongue in cheek. Moreover, he compared A. E. to Du Bellay and to Plutarch in his poem "To A. E. Going to America."[8]

But Gogarty was not the first to compare A. E. to Plato. In the little brochure, *The Irish Home Rule Convention*, John Quinn wrote from America: "Russell's *Thoughts for a Convention* has had a great effect on southern Unionist and Ulster opinion . . . . Seldom have I read a more eloquent and persuasive discussion of a great political question. Plato could not have done it better in the Athens of his day."[9] Literature was not John Quinn's profession, though he did what he could to foster the arts in Ireland by generous gifts, and he may be pardoned if his enthusiasm got out of bounds.

Stephen Gwynn after quoting from James Stephens' "Theme with Variations" said, "Just so one might have found in a Greek chorus a strophe in dispraise of love, answered by some resonant antistrophe."[10]

Yeats apparently fancied himself as consorting with reincarnated Greeks, for, according to Eglinton, he hailed his new ally, George Moore, when Moore returned to Ireland, as "the Aristophanes of Ireland."[11] Yeats thought of his own plays as emulating the Greek tragedy and said of *On Baile's Strand*, "I wanted to hear my own unfinished *Baile's Strand*, to hear Greek tragedy spoken with a Dublin accent."[12]

A. E. gives the key to understanding the spirit behind these comparisons. "Since the Greek civilization no European nation has had an intellectual literature which was genuinely national,"[13] he wrote. Dublin, intent upon making her country felt as a nation, was looking for a model of civic consciousness, a model whose awareness of nationality was a component of her artistic spirit. So it is that we find A. E. comparing Gogarty's lyrics to the Greek Anthology,[14] although Yeats, this time more modestly, is reminded by them of Fletcher and Herrick; and Colum attributes vast powers to A. E., who, he says, had "dared to make the obscure deities of Celtic mythology as potent as the Olympians."[15]

Although the Greeks were the preferred point of reference, Dante was not overlooked. James Joyce was commonly referred to as the "Dublin Dante." Eglinton repeats the sobriquet in his *Irish Literary Portraits*: "Our daemon, as Socrates pointed out, will only tell us what *not* to do, and if Joyce's daemon had made the mistake of saying to him in so many words, 'Thou shalt be the Dante of Dublin, a Dante with a difference it is true, as the Liffey is a more prosaic stream than the Arno: still, Dublin's Dante!' he might quite likely have drawn back and 'gone to the devil' with his fine tenor voice."[16] Eglinton makes a second reference: "Dublin has no quarrel with her Dante."[17] And yet again, "Still, a sensitive artist, reduced to impecunious despair as Joyce was at this period, might feel, in the very obscurity in which he was suffered to steal away out of Dublin, a sentence of banishment no less stern in its indifference than Florence's fiery sentence on her Dante."[18]

That Joyce was commonly so designated may be inferred from the tone of Gogarty's reference, when he spoke of Joyce's leaving Dublin. He said, "Dublin's Dante had to find a way out of his own Inferno."[19]

Colum felt that there was a physical resemblance between the two. He describes Joyce as "tall and slender . . . with a Dantesque face and steely blue eyes."[20]

Doubtless Joyce's exile, though self-imposed, prompted the comparisons in part. But an explanation for other Italian references does not so readily rise to mind. Synge, so George Moore says, was looked upon as an artist as great as Donatello or Benvenuto Cellini.[21] There seems to be considerable confusion in artistic media here. Perhaps there is more unity in Colum's reference to A. E.'s vision as "like the vision of Saint Theresa and William Blake and Michael Angelo."[22] St. John

Ervine outstripped all other references to the Italians when he declared A. E. to be almost as many-sided as Leonardo da Vinci.[23]

In such a mood the Dublin critic would not disregard Shakespeare. George Moore said very early that no dramatist other than Shakespeare and Yeats had succeeded in writing blank verse plays.[24] Gogarty puts the comparison into reverse: "How he [Shakespeare] escaped from being drawn into politics is a mystery. He must have been a kind of George Russell, one recognized as a literary man and one of whom politics is no more to be expected than meanness from a parish priest."[25]

Even the conservative Eglinton sees that Yeats had an advantage over Shakespeare:

. . . in *The Land of Heart's Desire* he had already succeeded in doing what the Shakespearian dramatists longed and tried unsuccessfully to do; and he was able to do so because that 'Celtic' element which survived in Shakespeare was the element in which Yeats moved with real power and understanding. In a word, Yeats had this advantage over Shakespeare, that he believed in the fairies; and though a belief in fairies is not a sufficiently central belief to serve a poet much in manipulating a drama of human destiny, yet in acquiescence in the supernatural was perhaps sufficiently characteristic of Irish writers to justify Yeats in his notable and bold design of founding a distinctive Irish drama.[26]

It seems curious that one could speak of *The Playboy of the Western World* and Shakespeare in a breath, but L. A. G. Strong wrote: "It [*The Playboy*] is an amazing piece of work, and the widespread realization that in no play outside of Shakespeare was such richness of language and variety to be found, is responsible for the wilder things that have been said about Synge; things which he would have been the first to disown with a smile."[27]

Not less bold is George Moore's reference to *Macbeth* and *Hamlet,* made in his preface to his friend Martyn's initial dramatic offering, *The Heather Field.* Moore said that Martyn's play would hold its own by the side of *The Wild Duck* or *Macbeth* or *Hamlet,* a curious juxtaposition of Ibsen and Shakespeare, moreover.[28] This reminds one of Moore's temerity, shown in an equally overwrought and inept comparison drawn between Yeats' *The Countess Cathleen* and Homer. Truly George Moore was running wild in his encomiums in this profuse preface:

> While he [Mr. Archer] was defending the indefensible . . . there was published unbeknown to him in London a play, beautiful as anything in Maeterlinck, a play possessing all the beauties of the Princess Maleine, and the beauty of verses equal to the verses of Homer. The name of this play is the "Countess Cathleen," and the name of its author is W. B. Yeats. If I had mentioned the name of a certain popular writer of military jargon our silly literary press would bubble with enjoyment, but the genius of W. B. Yeats, being a survival of that of the prophet and the seer of old time, escapes the appreciation of the newspapers.[29]

Colum pursues a curious logic while commending Yeats' desire for a theatre with which to inaugurate his epoch. Since Yeats was turning forty, Colum felt that it was time he had a theatre, for it was just at that age that Shakespeare, Goethe, and Ibsen had undertaken the production of plays in theatres under their own control.[30]

Other Elizabethans than Shakespeare were brought into focus as Colum compared Joyce's lyrics to the Elizabethan lyrics, asserting that in his opinion Joyce did not suffer by comparison. He judged Joyce's lyrics "quite as excellent."[31]

St. John Ervine, disagreeing with Stark Young's statement that Synge was following in the wake of D'Annunzio, declared that Synge was, rather, "a decadent descendant of the Elizabethans, more akin, perhaps, to Marlowe and Ford than to Shakespeare."[32]

The French also offered a fertile field for analogy and it was Eglinton who extolled Yeats' power of entering the esoteric world of Druidic magic without knowing a word of Gaelic, declaring that he was as learned in Celtic mythology "as ever was Ronsard in the mythologies of Greece and Rome."[33] Stephen Gwynn said that Hyde's play, *The Twisting of the Rope,* though a slight piece, would stand comparison with the proverbs of Musset or with Théodore de Banville's *Gringoire.*[34]

St. John Ervine defines at some length the manner in which Moore outstripped his master, Zola, in his novels:

One of his most remarkable novels, as it is also one of his earliest, "A Mummer's Wife," was clearly written under the influence of Zola, but with such individual quality that Zola might profitably have taken lessons from his pupil. The difference between Emile Zola and George Moore is that while Zola never forgot to be a doctrinaire, Moore never forgot to be an artist . . . . Zola made his novels out of things actually witnessed or learned from books, but Mr. Moore made his novels out of his own imagination. Zola could only write about life in a small shop in a small town after he had actually lived in it, but Mr. Moore wrote "A Mummer's Wife," with no more knowledge of Hanley than a person passing through it might possess, and gave his readers an impression of deep intimacy with it.[35]

By this time it would seem that the Irish may be all things at once, for such far-fetched comparisons are drawn as the likening of James Stephens' *In the Land of Youth* to the *Arabian Nights* to which, according to A. E., it is akin by virtue of its imagination.[36]

W. G. Fay in his memorial essay on Yeats called Yeats' *The Hour Glass* "the finest of all morality plays, with the possible exception of *Everyman*."[37] By the side of Fay, in the same volume, L. A. G. Strong said that the mind which Yeats' most resembled was Swift's, although the mind Yeats most desired to resemble was that of Blake. He said, furthermore, that in the poems, again and again, a terrible phrase recalled Swift's power.[38] Stephen Gwynn makes an interesting observation in the same connection: "He certainly never learnt to love the Irish people, but he learnt as Swift did, to be aware of their needs. Where Swift saw miserable poverty, Yeats saw intellectual starvation; and it was a purpose growing through his life to nourish the mind of Ireland."[39] Gwynn, in the same essay, compares Yeats to Milton, in that he was a dedicated person, self-appointed, and the only person comparable to Milton in his long and renewing growth.[40]

Joyce wrote of Yeats' "Adoration of the Magi" that it was "a story which one of the great Russians might have written."[41] The Russians are again brought to mind by A. E., who speaks of the quiet intensity of Colum's *Castle Conquer* and of its vivid pictures of Irish scenery and the Irish people who blend into that scenery "as artistically as the folk in Turgenieff's tales fit into the Russian steppes."[42]

Yeats weighed Lady Gregory's *Gods and Fighting Men* and *Cuchulain of Muirthemne* with Malory and felt "no discontent at the tally,"[43] while Stephen Gwynn compares her accomplishment with that of the Welshmen who handed down "The Mabinogion." Gwynn rather naïvely observes that "the task which Lady Gregory undertook was *not simply the task* of a scholar, which is to render fully the original, displaying the inherent imperfections."[44] Her task was rather to make those epics easy of enjoyment for the readers of today.

Rather more startling is Moore's eulogy of A. E., which should stand exactly as he set it down :"A. E.'s life is in his ideas as much as Christ's, and I will avouch that his wife has never tried to come between him and his ideas. As much cannot be said for Mary, whom Christ had to reprove for trying to dissuade him from his missions."[45]

It is only fair to say that some of the Irish critics noticed this overgenerosity in praise among their contemporaries. Katharine Tynan was aware of it: "We were terribly unexacting with ourselves in those days. We were appallingly easily satisfied with our achievements, as were our friends and critics. The amiable reviewers of the Dublin press, if they liked you, would salute your little work with a dreadful over-praise, likening you to shining ones of ancient and modern literature . . . . I myself have been compared to Sappho and St. Theresa in a breath."[46]

James Stephens, too, had his feet on the solid earth, as this note makes clear: "In referring to artists I do not here refer to Shakespeare or Dante or their peers. Such men stand above comparison or criticism, and possess a technic which lesser men can no more manipulate than they can play marbles with mountains."[47]

But however lightly one may be inclined to take certain of these comparisons, there is no room for doubt that, in the main, they were entertained seriously by the Irish critic. A. E. reveals the indisputable fact that the Irish reformers were looking for a Pericles, son of Patrick, and, fantastic as the idea may be, the proof that such an idea was consciously nourished is not difficult to find:

He [the Irish farmer] might be described almost as the primitive economic cave-man, the darkness of his cave unillumined by any ray of general principles . . . . His reading is limited to the local papers, and these, following the example of the modern press, carefully eliminate serious thought as likely to deprive them of readers. But Patrick, for all his economic backwardness, has a soul. The culture of the Gaelic poets and story-tellers, while not often actually remembered, still lingers like a fragrance about his mind. He lives and moves and has his being in the loveliest nature, the skies over him ever cloudy like an opal; and the mountains flow across his horizon in wave on wave of amethyst and pearl. He has the unconscious depth of character of all who live and labour much in the open air, in constant fellowship with the great companions—with the earth and the sky and the fire in the sky. We ponder over Patrick, his race and his country, brooding whether there is a seed of a Pericles in Patrick's loins. Could we carve an Attica out of Ireland?

Before Patrick can become the father of a Pericles, before Ireland can become an Attica, Patrick must be led out of his economic cave; his low cunning in barter must be expanded into a knowledge of economic law; his fanatical concentration on his family—begotten by the isolation and individualism of his life—be sublimed into national affections; his unconscious depths be sounded, his feelings for beauty be awakened by contact with some of the great literature of the world.[48]

Chapter VII
PERSONAL APPRAISALS

One of the most arresting statements made by Yeats in his *Autobiography* explains in a measure the highly personal tone of the criticism of the modern Irish school. Reflecting upon Moore's hypersensitivity toward public opinion, Yeats wrote: "If the National Theatre is ever started, what he is and what I am will be weighed, and very little what we have said or done."[1]

The writings of all the members of the coterie abound in personal commentary upon the appearance, mannerisms, habits, and character of these writers, with the result that the affinities and antipathies felt within the group are readily apparent. A. E. went so far as to define a literary movement as consisting of "five or six people who live in the same town and hate each other cordially."[2] It is singular that A. E. should have so emphasized the undeniable frictions that were no secret to the contemporary Irish public and which are profusely recorded in the Irish confessional literature, for he himself was the most unanimously admired and loved member of the group. He had even to protest to his friend George Moore that he had presented him as a plaster saint in *Hail and Farewell*.[3]

One can readily envisage all the leaders of the school, so frequently have their portraits been drawn by their contemporaries. In fact, it is almost impossible to disassociate the "master mystic,"[4] yet "bullockbefriending bard,"[5] A. E., from his beard and casual tweeds, or the poet Yeats from his swarthy skin, long hands, dangling forelock, and flowing tie. To think of Moore at all is to envisage a face lacking in contour, lacking in light and shadow, a face with a weak chin and pale-blue, wide-open eyes. The corpulent, short-sighted, bespectacled, pink-cheeked Martyn, the diminutive James Stephens, the long-faced, sandy-haired Gogarty, and Joyce with the sensitive mouth beneath the inscrutable eyes guarded by thick glass rise to mind at the mere mention of their names.

The temptation to wander at length in this portrait gallery is not easily resisted. There is a multiplicity of canvases before which one could pause, full-length studies, portrait busts, and miniatures. Of equal interest are those line drawings, where, by a few swift strokes, the underlying character of the sometimes unwilling subject is unmistakably revealed. Everywhere the character of the delineator, as well as that of the sitter, is swiftly communicated by the manner of his art.

The many descriptions of Yeats in his youth are adequately summarized in George Moore's portrait of Ulick Dean, which is obviously a literal description of Yeats, in Moore's *Evelyn Innes*:

> He had one of those long Irish faces, all in a straight line, with flat, slightly hollow cheeks, and a long chin. It was clean shaven and a heavy lock of hair was always falling over his eyes. It was his eyes that gave its sombre ecstatic character to his face. They were large, dark, deeply set, singularly shaped, and they seemed to smoulder like fires in caves, leaping and sinking out of the darkness. He was a tall, thin young man, and he wore a black jacket and a large, blue necktie, tied with the ends hanging loose over his coat.[6]

Later studies of Yeats emphasize a certain affectation of manner, a self-conscious pose in which his mannerism of priest-like gesture is noted. A summation of the descriptions of the aging Yeats, in which the oriental skin and grayed hair and large green-stoned ring are constant features, is offered by Gogarty in *Going Native,* a book in which the author employs a literal description of Yeats, whom he designates by name, as a springboard from which to plunge into a light-hearted fictional satire of English society. This projection of the real into the fictitious is characteristic of modern Irish literature, and however incongruous or incoherent the result of the method, future students of Yeats cannot but be grateful for Gogarty's picture of the poet. The lines run:

> Yeats . . . stood before me in his garden on the foothills of the Dublin Mountains. He stood tall and very stately as if his magnificent countenance was transfigured in the light. He raised his right arm in greeting and bowed his head in a way

suggestive of a strange resignation to my presence or to the interruption by the mundane of his communion with his kin in faeryland.[7] . . . The eagle face, aureoled by hair as white as the blossom of faery thorn, turned to me; his hand indicated a garden seat . . . . I looked closely at the face covered with its unageing ivory-brown skin and at the imperial brow so white and calm. His eyes were hard to catch directly. They were deep and bright, quick glancing as if a glance were all they needed for complete understanding of any mortal on whom they looked. I was filled with a strange eerie feeling of the supernatural as I sat by him . . . . There was something about him of the demigods . . . . He kept his head bowed, maintaining silence while his jeweled hand moved gently; then he said sorrowfully, "Grandeur is gone, Ouseley, grandeur is gone."[8]

An amusing action-picture of Yeats in his youth, in that period when he was engrossed, along with A.E., in theosophy, comes to us through the discerning care of Mrs. Kingsley Porter, who published the letters of A. E. to herself and to her husband. A. E. wrote to Mrs. Porter, reminiscing, in 1932: "I remember once quarreling with Yeats who was walking around the room with a sword in one hand muttering spells to ward off evil spirits and I noticed that every time he passed a plate of plums he put down his unoccupied hand and took a plum and I said, 'Yeats, you cannot evoke great spirits and eat plums at the same time,' and he insisted he could . . . . Yeats was in his youth when he ate the plums and has learned more about the fitness of things."[9]

Pictures of Yeats are seldom spiteful. However, George Moore, who could readily toss off a caricature, referred to Yeats' height and "hierarchic appearance" as authorizing his dogmatic pronouncements and declared that he was the most complete type of "literary fop" that had ever appeared in literature.[10]

Moore's descriptions of other members of the school are equally revelatory of Moore's own nature. He said that Hyde inspired a sort of revulsion in him, and that he "looked like an imitation native Irish speaker; in other words like a stage-Irishman." Moore had noted that all Hyde's head seemed at the back, like that of a walrus.[11]

Moore had a trick of seeming to write a complimentary description of a character and of then damning the whole by some derogatory epithet or scurrilous phrase at the end. For example, he wrote of Lady Gregory as "a middle-aged woman, agreeable to look upon, perhaps for her broad, handsome, intellectual brow enframed in iron-gray hair. The brown, wide-open eyes are often lifted in looks of appeal and inquiry, and a natural wish to sympathize softens her voice till it whines."[12] After remarking that her eyes were always full of questions, Moore said that her Protestant high school air became her greatly but estranged him from her.[13]

Moore associated John Eglinton's physical appearance with his style of writing, saying that the man's writings were "gnarled and personal" like the man himself.[14] He described Eglinton as "a thin small man with dark red hair growing stiffly over a small skull." He studied his "round head and high forehead, and the face somewhat shriveled and thickly freckled," and reflected that his appearance betokened the gnarled, solitary life of the bachelor. He compared him to a thorn tree that breaks into flower, for he argued "in a thorny, tenacious way," but he wrote beautiful prose.[15]

Moore explained to his readers that he had included no personal description of A. E. in *Hail and Farewell* because he existed "in one's sentiments and feelings rather than in one's ordinary sight" and because "the fleeting outlines" always escaped him. He said that all he could remember was "the long, gray, pantheistic eyes that looked so often into my soul with such a kindly gaze."[16]

It was such remarks that A. E. objected to, but he was amused by James Stephens' reference to him in *The Charwoman's Daughter*. Lucy Kingsley Porter in her introduction to *A. E.'s Letters to Minánlabáin* says: "He chuckled and asked me to tell Holmes how James Stephens had described him in *The Charwoman's Daughter*, 'There was a tall man with a sweeping brown beard whose heavy overcoat looked as though it had been put on with a shovel.' "[17] In Susan Mitchell's description of him, the emphasis is, once more, on A. E.'s careless dress:

. . . He needed clothes and never bought them. His best coat was all rags, with the pockets burned out by his pipes. Instead of putting the arms through the sleeves, as any sane man would do to keep the wind and rain from his back, he slings it cape-wise over his shoulders, and very often lets it slip behind him in the dust and mud. He is careless, stupid about himself and his requirements, untidy, but—

Ah, well, he's A. E., and that's all there's to it. You can't be cross with him. He is a child.[18]

Padraic Colum, kinder than Moore in his description of Douglas Hyde, stressed the dignity of the then newly inaugurated President of Eire: "President Hyde is now approaching his eightieth year. I remember him as having hair that was literally as black as a raven's ·wing, with a drooping black mustache. His is a swarthy face, square, with marked cheek bones and faintly colored eyes. Now his hair and mustache are white and his figure gaunt. But with that heavy head, those aboriginal features, he looks like a man belonging to some ancient ruling people."[19]

Yeats and Martyn repaid Moore in kind and penned representations of the more eminent caricaturist that are vivid, at least; and the more tolerant, because the less abused, Gogarty has given posterity a few lines from which it is easy to fill out the suggestion. Yeats tells us that "Moore's body was insinuating, upflowing, circulative, curvicular, pop-eyed,"[20] while Gogarty refers to him as "pink and white as a Dresden shepherd."[21] Martyn's revenge has been but briefly circulated. He caricatured Moore in a play, *The Dream Physician,* under the slightly altered name of George Augustus Moon. The hero of the play, Moon, is described in the stage directions as plump of body, with "short thick legs, very broad hips, very sloping shoulders, a long neck and a pasty, almost featureless face." His facial expression is one of "absent-mindedness and vacuity."[22] Martyn's accent on Moore's effeminacy is his countercharge against Moore's repetitious emphasis on Martyn's celibacy.

Eglinton, in a matter-of-fact way, reports of Moore a curious fact, which he said that no one would suspect, namely, that Moore had "the proper use of only one eye."[23]

James Joyce has left the most economical yet the most indelible impressions of the physical appearance of the writers of the Dublin school. Surrealistic, one might say of such lines as "Eglintoneyes, quick with pleasure, looked up shybrightly. Gladly glancing, a merry puritan, through the twisted Eglantine";[24] or of his reference to Gogarty's "shaking gurgling face . . . equine in its length" and his "light untonsured hair, grained and hued like pale oak."[25] He speaks of Gogarty's "well-fed voice"[26] and remarks that "he clasped his paunchbrow."[27] His descriptions of Gogarty (as Buck Mulligan, of course) are climaxed with the reference to "the primrose elegance and town bred manners of Malachai Roland St. John Mulligan."[28]

Joyce gives us A. E. as one of the "opal hush" poets, with mocking references to his vegetarianism and his studies of Brahman theosophy: ". . . The high figure in homespun, beard and bicycle, a listening woman at his side. Coming from the vegetarian. Only weggebobbles and fruit. Don't eat a beefsteak. If you do the eyes of that cow will pursue you through eternity."[29]

From Joyce one hears that A. E. "oracled out of his shadow," and again one sees "a tall figure in bearded homespun" as it "rose from the shadow and unveiled its co-operative watch."[30]

These examples of portraiture must suffice. It is evident that Moore, Yeats, and A. E., all of whom had studied art and had essayed their skill as painters, exercised the seeing eye of the portraitist, while Joyce had that inexplicable power of genius which enabled him to give life to a figure by a decidedly limited number of strokes.

The method of personal evaluation apart from the conjuring up of the physical presence, as instanced above, is nowhere better illustrated in Irish criticism than in the continuously recurring comment upon the "aloofness" of the poet Yeats. This quality of his temperament is alluded to by a varied terminology, such as his aristocracy, hauteur, superiority, inhumanity, arrogance, or stoicism. It is now deplored, now condemned, yet often condoned. It is occasionally denied.

All his associates sought to explain it, and Yeats himself frequently analyzes the trait and leaves no one in doubt that he deliberately fostered it for a purpose.

John Eglinton said that Yeats was "born into a natural sense of aristocracy" and that he had inherited from his father "a strong feeling of superiority."[31] It mattered not that his father was an impoverished artist. The Yeats family were the aristocrats of the little patriarchal village of Sligo.

Stephen Gwynn notes that Yeats' "arrogance" had denied him a "ready audience in Ireland." The manner in which Yeats denounced to the young men of Dublin the old poets whom they had admired roused in these youths an antagonism and left to Yeats the task of succeeding with the few. It "is a notable example," wrote Gwynn, "of what can be done by disregarding the many."[32] But Gwynn defended Yeats' arrogance: "The greatest service that Yeats rendered to Ireland was his persistent refusal to accept as admirable anything that was commended solely by patriotic or virtuous intention. He taught Ireland the value of a certain intellectual arrogance, a contempt for the standards of the crowd."[33] Gwynn, in his autobiography, relates an anecdote about a lack of compassion shown toward Lady Margaret Sackville's coachman on the part of that lady, and concludes with the statement that Yeats himself would have been equally uncompassionate. "Perhaps a certain hardness goes into the making of a poet," he remarked.[34]

St. John Ervine also made mention of Yeats' effect on young men. He goes so far as to call his diffidence "unhumanity": "His effect on young men is peculiar. His brilliant conversation is very attractive to them, but his insensibility to the presence of human beings repels them . . . . Mr. Yeats has something of the unhumanity of Mr. Griffith. His talk is brilliant, indeed, but it is not comradely talk. It never lapses from high quality to the easy familiarities which harmonize all relationships . . . . He is one of the loneliest men in the world, for he cannot express himself except in a crowd."[35]

Yeats' aloofness seems to be a particularly sore point with Ervine. His feeling arose in part, no doubt, from his unhappy experience with the Abbey Theatre actors who, during Ervine's brief directorship, rebelled against Ervine's tyranny. By Yeats' prompt action the distressing connection was speedily terminated. Hence it is no wonder that Ervine should have focused his attention on what he considered the tragic flaw in Yeats' character. Yeats appeared to Ervine as pontifical in conversation: "It is not easy to talk to him in a familiar fashion, and I imagine that he has difficulty in talking easily on common topics. I soon discovered that he is not comfortable with individuals: he needs an audience to which he can discourse in a pontifical manner . . . . His talk is seldom about commonplace things: it is either in a high and brilliant style or else it is full of reminiscences of dead friends. I do not believe that anyone in this world has ever spoken familiarly to him."[36]

Again, Ervine said that Yeats' aloofness differed from that of Galsworthy, who was "perturbed about mankind," for Yeats was, he said, "totally unconcerned about problems of any sort."[37] He seems loath to drop his theme and returns to it later: "It may be that Mr. Yeats's aloofness from men is due to the fact that he thinks too much and feels too little."[38]

George Moore has given us a vivid picture of Yeats' indifference of manner in the character of Ulick Dean in *Evelyn Innes*. Ulick is calling upon Evelyn: "He shook hands with her vaguely, and sat down on a Sheraton chair and fixed his eyes on the Aubusson carpet. She thought for some time that he was examining it, but at last the truth dawned; he did not see it all, he was maybe a thousand years away, lost in some legendary past . . . he answered her questions perfunctorily, and without any apparent reason he got up and walked about the room; but not looking at any object as he walked about, with hanging head, absorbed in thought."[39]

Frank O'Connor describes Yeats in maturity as "masterful and intolerant" in committee, "sifting words and chopping logic. He was a tyrant who used his position shamelessly to get his own way."[40]

Joseph Hone in his biography of the poet accents the trait of "aloofness," interpreting it as a feeling of class-consciousness. Yeats' native bent was encouraged, he said, by his tour of Italy with Lady Gregory. "He came home," writes Hone, "to lecture on the 'immoral Irish bourgeoisie' without past and without discipline, to which Ireland was surrendering her soul."[41]

Lady Gregory records Yeats' attitude at this time as set forth in his letter to her in which he expresses some despair over the mob: "Mr. Yeats wrote: 'Here we are, a lot of intelligent people who might have been doing some sort of decent work that leaves the soul free; yet here we are, going through all sorts of trouble and annoyance for a mob that knows neither literature nor art. I might have been away in the country, in Italy, perhaps, writing poems for my equals and my betters.' "[42]

In a passage addressed to the "slum snob," Gogarty wittily presents his own theory of the pre-eminence of the aristocratic type over every other form of humanity, concluding, "But a man must have some opinions of his own even in Ireland, if he is to retain his individuality, or any individuality at all. And my opinion is that a good aristocrat is the highest type that humanity or evolution has evolved."[43]

It is not surprising that a man of such opinion should have written sympathetically of Yeats as an Apollo among herdsmen. "What a tragedy it was," he wrote, "for the golden dreamer awakened from the creative dream of his that turned his country into a faery land . . . to be confronted rudely by the worthlessness and worldliness of his countrymen. The poet disillusioned had become a Stoic."[44]

In an essay designed to stand as one of several tributes in an elegiac collection, Maud Gonne does not avoid what she considers the fact of his class-consciousness. Maud Gonne had lived to see a lover's devotion turn to disdain, after long years of public acknowledgment through lyrical expression. Her criticism leaves the reader in little doubt of its justice, but, under the circumstances, in considerable doubt as to its good taste: "He [Yeats] found himself among the comfortable and well-fed, who style themselves the 'upper classes,' but whom Willie, shuddering at the words . . . called Distinguished Persons . . . . The Abbey and its peasant plays catered for their amusement; but Willie's own plays were seldom performed there because he could not write down to their level, and concealed the fact from himself by saying that the actors could not act up to his."[45]

F. R. Higgins, in the same collection of complimentary essays, supports this conception of Yeats' contempt for the "middle minds":

His poetry never saw eye to eye with the middle classes. The bloodlessness, the loose sentiment of middle-minded verse, was to him an abhorrence. There were for him, only two commingling states of verse. One, simple, bucolic, or Rabelaisian, the other, intellectual, exotic, or visionary. The middle minds lacked distinction, poise; he had little interest or patience with them. To them his poetry may seem a beautiful secretion from a mind of aristocratic pedantry in which the insignificant is given an absurdly pontifical importance. Above them Yeats, however, nobly asserted his aloofness, striking home with a more telling, naked enterprise in Irish song —until he retired, as it were, into his own shell, but from there we hear the almost imperceptible music of a lost Kingdom.[46]

A. E., in a review of Yeats' *Autobiography*, complained that the poet had revealed too little of his inner life. "I hold that there is only one person that man may know intimately, and that is himself. If he be a man of genius, what he could tell us about his own inner life would be of much more value than anything he could tell us of the external life of others," said A. E. He added that the biography reminded him of a many-colored shell from which the creature who had once lived in it had slipped away, "leaving only the miracle of form to wonder at."[47] Thus A. E. accused Yeats of being aloof even in his most personal utterance.

L. A. G. Strong and Lennox Robinson roundly deny that Yeats was aloof and incapable of warmth. Strong says that it was a popular delusion that grew into a legend that Yeats "felt very keenly." Strong declares that he was friendly and sociable, but that "unless a person were very tongue-tied, young and unhappy, Yeats lacked the gift for making overtures."[48] Yeats, according to Strong, had been impressed by

Goethe's apothegm in *Wilhelm Meister,* "The poor are; the rich are enabled also to seem." He quotes Yeats as having said that when he read that line he was himself shy and awkward and that he had then set himself to acquire this technique of seeming. "I forced myself to attend functions of every kind until I had it." Thus he had a public manner which was projected, but not insincere.[49]

Lennox Robinson says that "in dealing with inferiors there was no arrogance, no consciousness of superiority" on Yeats' part. "He loathed pretentiousness in others and so had none himself." Evidently this legend hounded Yeats to his grave, for Robinson says that in some obituary notice he was described as unapproachable and that the writer of the notice had said that no one outside his family ever called him by his Christian name.[50]

An overwhelming number of references to this single trait of Yeats are readily available. For such as appear here we find thirteen authors: Eglinton, Stephen Gwynn, Ervine, Moore, O'Connor, Hone, Lady Gregory, Gogarty, Maud Gonne, F. R. Higgins, A. E., L. A. G. Strong, and Lennox Robinson. It seems appropriate at this point to hear how the poet himself explained this personality trait which, among his critics, overshadowed all others in interest. He speaks of his silence as an acquired trait:

> I was at Sligo when I received a letter from John O'Leary, saying that I could do no more in Dublin, for even the younger men had turned against me, were "jealous," his letter said, though what they had to be jealous of God knows. He had said further that it was all my own fault, that he had warned me what would happen if I lived on terms of intimacy with those I tried to influence. I should have kept myself apart and alone. It was all true; through some influence from an earlier generation, from Walt Whitman, perhaps, I had sat talking in public bars, had talked late into the night at many men's houses, showing all my convictions to men that were but ready for one, and used conversation to explore and discover among men who looked for authority. I did not yet know that intellectual freedom and social equality are incompatible; and yet, if I had, could hardly have lived otherwise, being too young for silence.[51]

As for his sense of aristocracy, he wrote: "Ireland has grown sterile, because power has passed to certain men who lack the training which requires a certain amount of wealth to ensure continuity from generation to generation, and to free the mind in part from other tasks. A gentleman is a man whose principal ideas are not connected with his personal needs and his personal success. In old days he was a clerk or a noble, that is to say, he had freedom because of inherited wealth and position, or because of a personal renunciation."[52]

He looked upon silence as a means of strength and admired Synge and Lady Gregory because they had the power to isolate themselves, Synge instinctively, and Lady Gregory by taking thought. He reproached himself for being too talkative and said that "one must agree with the clown or be silent, for he has in him the strength and the confidence of multitudes."[53]

Yeats confessed that all his life he had been haunted by the idea that he should know all classes of men as one of themselves and that he should combine the greatest possible personal realization with the greatest possible knowledge of the speech and circumstances of the world. He had even thought of wandering in the West of Ireland disguised as a peasant and of shipping as a sailor. But he had never acquired the courage to venture forth. Finally he came to rest on the conclusion that "the artist grows more and more distinct, more and more a being in his own right as it were, but more and more loses grasp of the always more complex world."[54]

In his letters he frequently spoke of his purposeful isolation. To Katharine Tynan he wrote when he was young: "I hate journalists. There is nothing in them but tittering, jeering emptiness. They have all made what Dante calls the Great Refusal,—that is they have ceased to be self-centered, have given up their individuality."[55]

As an aging man he wrote to Dorothy Wellesley concerning his proposed trip to Majorca that the very fact that he was going with a man whose mind he could touch at only one point meant peace. "I can live in my own mind and write poetry; can go into a dream and stay there," he said.[56] A few days later he wrote: "I am planning a new life, four months in every year in some distant spot and nothing to do but poetry—the rest of the year mainly in Dublin and work for my family . . . . My public life I will pare down to almost nothing. My imagination is on fire again."[57]

That public encroachments upon the poet were a source of pain to him is evidenced in a letter to Dorothy Wellesley wherein he explains that during a period of concentration on writing he was "like those people in a religious meditation who if you lay a finger on an arm show a bruise where you touched them." He had hoped to go to Penns in the Rocks, the country home of Lady Wellesley, for there he thought he could "escape this touch" on his arm.[58]

This aloofness, then, was the personality trait of Yeats most remarked upon by the Irish critics. It would be possible to treat each member of the modern Irish school in the same fashion. One could assemble a mass of comment upon Moore's pose of the roué, or upon the wit and broad speech of Gogarty, who is said to have walked through Dublin shedding limericks as he went, or on the aggressive manner of Lady Gregory, on the volubility of A. E., and so on through a round of observations that are a far cry from the exaggerated praise so liberally given when any one of the number was launching a play or a novel or a collection of poems.

The critics' personalizing of the character by describing the physical appearance and by accenting striking personal traits reveals where the affinities and antipathies lie, for the tone of the comment gives the broad hint. But one need not depend on mere suggestion, since the critics have provided their readers with an abundance of plain and direct statements relative to the harmony and hostility that existed within the group. These assertions may now be considered.

Chapter VIII
AFFINITIES AND ANTIPATHIES

A. E. once said to Kingsley Porter in a letter that "the trouble about literary movements in any country is this that there are only two or three writers of genius and they generally hate each other because they see different eternities."[1] Yet of all the individuals who formed the literary coterie of modern Ireland the one least prone to stimulate animosity was A. E. Perhaps the strange mixture of hard-headedness and romantic mysticism within his own character enabled him to meet sympathetically a wider range of temperament than others of his associates were able to comprehend. Frank O'Connor contrasts him with Yeats, who was, he said, "subtle, casuistical, elegant, mannered; a diplomat who had flattered rich and brilliant women into serving his cause." A. E., on the other hand, was "guileless" and "full of universal benevolence."[2]

It is generally known that Yeats and A. E. were close friends, but it is less popularly understood that there was from time to time friction between them. At the time of A. E.'s death Yeats wrote to Lady Wellesley: "A. E. was my oldest friend. I constantly quarreled with him but he never bore malice, and in his last letter to me, a month before his death, he said that generally when he differed from me it was that he feared to be absorbed by my personality."[3]

This explanation is somewhat complimentary to Yeats. There is evidence of more specific cause for the disagreements that frequently arose between them. For example, when Yeats was in London as a young man he associated himself briefly with the magazine, *The Savoy*. A. E. called *The Savoy* "the organ of the incubi and succubi"[4] and wrote a letter to Yeats remonstrating with him for selling his birthright for a mess of pottage. It was Synge's knowledge of this difference of opinion, or taste, that led him to write to Stephen MacKenna, "It would be a mistake to send your manuscript to Yeats and A. E., as what one likes the other hates."[5]

A more serious difference of opinion arose over the question of A. E.'s encouragement of the young poet, James Stephens. Yeats grudgingly heard A. E. read the poems of his protégé and when A. E. spoke of his hope of seeing them published, Yeats said, if George Moore's record may be trusted, "For me the aesthetical question; for you, my dear friend, the philanthropic."[6] Yeats was implying that A. E.'s sympathies were getting the better of him, and was affirming that his own judgment of a young poet would rest solely on tested aesthetic criteria. A. E. was hurt by Yeats' attitude, but was not the less confident of his young poet friend, James Stephens.

Yeats' attitude toward A. E.'s fostering of James Stephens, and likewise of Padraic Colum, continued to be supercilious, and he remarked to Lord Dunsany, who had offered A. E. a small sum for founding a review, "I see that you are going to offer groundsel for A. E.'s canaries." According to George Moore the sneer that accompanied the remark brought the project to naught.[7]

When Yeats finally acknowledged the literary gifts of James Stephens, his earlier attitude was so generally known as to leave him suspect when he essayed a public compliment. Shaw Desmond records such an instance: "It was Yeats, I think, who, in making a presentation to the author of 'The Crock of Gold,' said something to this effect: 'It gives me great pleasure to make this presentation, as we all know that my friend, James Stephens, will go down in history as a great poet.' The feelings of Stephens, who is essentially a prose writer, may be easily imagined and are therefore indescribable."[8]

Yeats' attitude may well have been annoying to A. E., who was justifiably proud of his discovery of Stephens. George Moore recounts the occasion of their meeting. A. E., having recognized in the newspaper verse of Stephens a new songster, "put on his hat and went away with his cage, discovering him in a lawyer's office." Moore describes their meeting and the result. He reveals that Yeats was not alone in his feeling that A. E. was pushing his claims for his novice a bit too hard:

. . . A great head and two soft brown eyes looked at him over a typewriter, and an alert and intelligent voice asked him whom he wanted to see. A. E. said that he was looking for James Stephens, a poet, and the typist answered: "I am he." And the next Sunday evening he was admitted to the circle, and we were impressed by his wit and whimsicality, but we thought A. E. exaggerated the talents of the young man . . . . It was clear that he was anxious to put this new man alongside of Synge, and that we would not consent to do.[9]

Yeats writes with extreme candor in his *Autobiography* regarding his feelings toward A. E. at the time when A. E.'s *Deirdre* was being staged at the Abbey Theatre.[10] Yeats did not like the play, which he thought A. E. had written as a protest against his own and Moore's *Diarmuid and Grania.* A. E. had said that the product of that collaboration was objectionable because it had made mere men out of heroes and he was evidently setting up a model for the treatment of the Gaelic legendary hero. Yeats said that he disliked A. E.'s *Deirdre,* but was troubled by the fear that he was reacting from prejudice, for, he confessed, "then as always," he loved and hated A. E. and he distrusted his own judgment, "fearing it were jealousy, or some sort of party dislike."[11]

It may well have been jealousy, for he spoke of the popularity of *Deirdre* with the crowd, when reporting progress at the theatre to Lady Gregory, who was then in Italy. Two days later he wrote her again, and his observations reach an astonishing conclusion: "The plays are over. Last night was the most enthusiastic of all. The audience now understands *Cathleen ni Houlihan* and there is no difficulty in getting from humour to tragedy. There is continued applause, and *strange to say I like Deirdre.*"[12]

Was it so "strange"? It seems obvious that the play which he had condemned two days previously as "superficial and sentimental"[13] had now leapt into favor because his own play was at last sharing the applause.

It was Gogarty's opinion that Yeats and A. E. "blended badly."[14] If so, the reason lay not so much in their disparate ideals or interests as in Yeats' singularity, or in his natural instinct to preserve the citadel of his own soul from any and all infringements and encroachments from without. It was not Yeats' disposition to "blend" with anybody. His feeling for A. E. was in the main friendly, and, as he himself said, he counted him ever as a friend in spite of their constant quarrels. That the friendship endured probably rested on the fact, which Yeats admitted, that A. E. never bore malice.

It was an accomplishment of a sort on A. E.'s part that he should have been consistently and continuously eulogized by George Moore, who customarily spared neither friend nor foe. And yet Moore once wrote a damaging line about A. E.: ". . . When John [Eglinton] bade me good-bye at the door he admonished me to be very careful what I said about A. E.'s home life."[15]

This and no more. Could volumes have said more or been so subtly damaging? Moore's devotion to A. E. was real and of longer duration than was usual with the fickle novelist, but he was likewise an incorrigible gossip and could not resist an allusion to a mild bit of scandal breathed in Dublin at the time.[16] It is only fair to remember that Moore, in writing of A. E., repeatedly praised him. "It is a great good fortune," he wrote, "to have a friend whose eyes light up always when they see one, and whose mind stoops or lifts itself instinctively to one's trouble, divining it, whether it be spiritual or material."[17]

Moore felt a kinship with A. E., whatever casual observers thought of their likeness or dissimilarity: "I rose from my seat, and looked round, thinking that in A. E. as in myself thought and action are at one. We are alike in essentials, though to the casual observer regions apart . . . . But everybody in Dublin thinks that he is like A. E., as everybody in the world thinks he is like Hamlet."[18]

But Moore could ill brook any adverse criticism of his writing and so it came about that he fell out with the man of whom he had said: "Were the moon to drop out of the sky the nights would be darker, but Dublin without A. E. would be like the sky without a sun in it."[19] Moore had written to A. E. of *The Brook Kerith*, "You will like this the best of my books," to which Russell replied, "On the contrary, I like it the least of your books." And then, according to Frank O'Connor, A. E. had continued with a jocular comment: "Jesus did at least convert the world, but your Jesus wouldn't convert an Irish Board of Guardians." After this incident, says O'Connor, "there was silence between them for many years." He finishes off his story as follows: "In old age they were reconciled, and Russell went to dine in Ebury Street. The two cronies gossiped all the evening about Dublin days, avoiding all reference to 'The Brook Kerith.' But as Russell walked away from the door, Moore shouted after him, 'You wanted Jesus to be clever.'

" 'No, Moore, merely intelligent,' A. E. called back."[20]

Intimate bits are on record concerning A. E.'s relationships with other members of the school. Stephen Gwynn refers to him as the "singular and much beloved man of genius," and as "the easiest and friendliest creature in the world to talk to."[21] Reference has already been made to the use Gwynn made of A. E. in his novel, *The Old Knowledge*. A. E. had been pleased and he wrote to Gwynn to tell him that he did not mind the slight use Gwynn had made of him as copy: "I have grown accustomed to it. Yeats began it and George Moore completed my education in this way. Nobody will ever know and it does not matter. I was thinking it would help the sale of The Secret Rose, the Celtic Twilight, Evelyn Innes and Sister Teresa, and The Old Knowledge if I brought action for libel against you all. After deducting expenses we could share profits on increased sales. I see infinite possibilities of amusement in this way."[22]

By this we see that A. E. was the subject of fictionalized portraits in five books, by his own acknowledgment. His pleasure over his being alluded to in Stephens' *The Charwoman's Daughter* has previously been mentioned. Katharine Tynan says that James Stephens was poking sly, loving fun at A. E. in the talking Philosopher in *The Crock of Gold*. According to Mrs. Hinkson (Katharine Tynan) the three greatest talkers in Dublin were A.E., Stephen MacKenna, and James Stephens himself.[23] James Joyce records A. E.'s conversations liberally in *Ulysses*. Frank O'Connor once teased A. E. about Joyce's having made him say that "the supreme question about a work of art is out of how deep a life does it spring."[24] A. E. had seemed surprised and had exclaimed, "Well, that's very clever of him! . . . That's true, you know. I may quite well have said that!" And O'Connor adds that he said it at least once every day.[25] It is characteristic of Joyce to have linked together for all time the man and his bromide.

No matter how far one goes in assembling comment regarding A. E., one comes out with the indelible impression of the geniality of the man's nature. Therefore it does not surprise one to hear of A. E.'s confessing to a desire to shock his public, for no man of vigor cares to be considered the chocolate-coated hero. A. E. wrote to Yeats, "I think you will like my articles on Celtic mythology when they appear . . . . When I think of the people I will annoy I grow cheerful and write better."[26]

Yeats was aloof; A. E., warmly responsive and genial; George Moore, cantankerous. Yeats' associates, for the most part, accepted him at his own evaluation of himself. A. E. got on smoothly with all Dublin. Moore was constantly embroiled in quarrels.[27]

Among Moore's relationships none is more interesting than that which developed between him and Lady Gregory. Moore was plainly jealous of Yeats' place in Lady Gregory's regard. He had been drawn into association with the two of them when he became one of the directors of the Irish Literary Theatre. He had accepted their invitation to join with them in the project in order to attract publicity for himself. He says in *A Communication to My Friends* that "despite the success of *Evelyn Innes* I began to perceive that my name had disappeared from the columns of the daily and weekly press. My books were reviewed, but my public was not nourished like that of other authors by descriptions of my personal life."[28]

Moore, then, became closely associated with Yeats and Lady Gregory. In *Ave* he writes of his communing with himself regarding their mutual relationships: " 'She has been wise all her life through,' I said; 'she knew him [Yeats] to be her need at once, and she never hesitated . . . yet she knew me before she knew him.' "29

In *Vale* Moore wrote: "He [Yeats] was ever looking for disciples, and sought them in vain till he met Lady Gregory."30 He finally rebuked Yeats for his air of proprietorship with Lady Gregory, spoke in an uncomplimentary fashion of that lady, and left Yeats overwhelmed: " 'One thing, Yeats, I have always had in mind but never liked to tell you; it is that the way you come down the steps from the stage and stride up the stalls and alight by Lady Gregory irritates the audience, and if you will allow me to be perfectly frank, I will tell you that she is a little too imposing, too suggestive of Corinne or Madame de Staël.'

". . . and Yeats went away overwhelmed and I saw no more of him for many months."31 When these remarks are placed beside his anecdote involving Sir Edwin Arnold it seems clear that Moore was jealous of his standing with Lady Gregory: "When Sir Edwin rose to go she produced a fan and asked him to write his name upon one of the sticks. But she did not ask me to write my name, though at that time I had written not only 'A Modern Lover,' but also 'A Mummer's Wife,' and I left the house feeling for the first time that the world I lived in was not so profound as I had imagined it to be."32

Those who have no more than a casual acquaintance with the Irish Revival are informed as to Moore's attitude toward Yeats as revealed in *Hail and Farewell*. Typical of his contemptuous remarks is this, from *Vale*: "In writing *Patience*, Gilbert thought he was copying Oscar Wilde, whereas he was drawing Willie Yeats out of the womb of Time."33

Moore complained that in his conversations with Yeats the latter never attended to what Moore was saying and always brought the conversation back to what interested him. He complained also that Yeats' manner in conversation was too dignified.34 An egoist himself, he was acutely aware of the condescension of the self-centered Yeats.

Lady Gregory said that she had "no feeling against Mr. Moore because of what he had said about her in his trilogy," but she said that she "could never forgive the insults it contained to Mr. Yeats."[35] She never actively retaliated in print, but Yeats several times evened the score, notably in his little skit, "The Cat and the Moon." In *Plays and Controversies* Yeats had said that Moore was a very vivid character and that he was precisely one of those who could most easily be represented on the stage. However, Yeats never made a prolonged study of that "headlong, intrepid man"[36] for dramatic purposes. In his preface to "The Cat and the Moon" in *Wheels and Butterflies* Yeats wrote: " 'The holy man in the big house' . . . and his friend from Mayo were meant for Edward Martyn and George Moore, both of whom were living when the play was written. I think the audience understood the reference."[37]

And well they might, for the reference is unmistakable, pointing as it does to that pose of George Moore's heretofore mentioned, the pose of the roué:

Blind Beggar: . . . Did you ever know a holy man but had a wicked man for his comrade and heart's darling? There is not a more holy man in the barony than the man who has the big house at Laban, and he goes knocking about the roads day and night with that old lecher from the county of Mayo and he a woman hater from the day of his birth. And well you know and well the neighbors know what they talk of by daylight and candlelight. The old lecher does be telling over all the sins he committed, or maybe never committed at all, and the man of Laban does be trying to head him off and quiet him down that he may quit telling them.[38]

In the section of his autobiography entitled "Dramatis Personae" Yeats adopts Moore's own method, casting all dignity aside in order to depreciate the novelist:

He reached to middle life ignorant of even small practical details. He said to a friend: "How do you keep your pants from falling about your knees?" "Oh," said the friend, "I put my braces through the little tapes that are sewn there for the purpose." A few days later he thanked the friend with emotion. Upon a long country bicycle ride with another friend, he had stopped because his pants were about his knees, had gone behind a hedge, had taken them off, and exchanged them at a cottage for a tumbler of milk.[39]

Yeats goes into great detail about Moore's quarrels with

his cooks and with his neighbors. He ridicules Moore's inaccurate French, his ignorance of Shakespeare, his failure to attain a disciplined style. He concedes that as a country gentleman Moore dressed the part. In fact "no Mayo county gentleman had ever dressed the part so well." Although "he lacked manners," he "had manner."[40] The comment on his manners should not have troubled Moore, who had said previously, "Well-mannered people do not think sincerely, their minds are full of evasions and subterfuges."[41]

Yeats, writing of Moore in a letter to A. E., who was later to be Moore's chief Dublin friend, wrote a comparison of himself and Moore as opposites. Yeats said that he understood people and sympathized with all kinds of character more easily than did Moore. He thought he was more tolerant than Moore who, he said, understood nobody but himself. This lack of understanding led Moore to be "always condemning or worshipping." He granted that Moore understood ideas, but thought that his powers of judgment did not embrace human nature.[42]

Lennox Robinson compares the two as conversationalists. He pictures them at supper together in London during a period of mutual hostility. "It was delightful to sit back and listen to Moore fumbling for the retort that was to annihilate; but before the right words could be found Yeats had presented some other facet of the subject, leaving Moore floundering in the background."[43]

Moore returned from London to Dublin shortly after the Easter Rebellion of 1916, and during his visit he asked St. John Ervine to assist him toward a reconciliation with Yeats and Lady Gregory, but although Ervine proposed to them that they "should pool their pardons" and receive Moore into the fold again, his proposal was not accepted.[44]

When Yeats wrote that it was "Moore's own fault that everybody hated him except a few London painters,"[45] he was somewhat excessive. True, James Stephens "froze"[46] at the mention of Moore, and Gogarty called him "the most potentially cantankerous man one could meet," but Moore had eloquent defenders, among them Gogarty, who said that Moore's detachment was such that he could describe all his acquaintances objectively and include himself in the pageant.[47] Gogarty records that in discussions with Yeats he had defended him as a great artist, and continues: "He was a great person and he never forgot it. His air of perpetual cantankerousness was to defend himself from rational little critics 'while the work was in progress'; to defend himself from reality and common-sense. Had he not said, 'We must keep up the illusion'? And while he attended to his garden, the garden of his prose, he resented what anyone can have if they hear fools gladly—comments."[48]

Moore's biographer, Joseph Hone, says that "it would be wrong to think that Moore was cold-shouldered in Dublin." His social life was not curtailed, according to Hone, by his mordant temper.[49]

Ervine defends him. But Ervine, of course, had not been used as a target in *Hail and Farewell*. He does what he can to dissolve "the legend" that Moore was "immensely egotistical" and that he had the "simplicity of the buffoon." Ervine commended him as "an audacious, exceedingly adroit and utterly unthwartable artist";[50] his simplicity was not that of the buffoon, but was that simplicity of character which is so frequently inherent in the man of genius.

John Eglinton called Moore a "pathetically lonely figure" and "a notable example of stoic fortitude." He describes him as expert in tête-à-tête and his humor as "a sudden flash of veracity." Eglinton did not mind Moore's "peering curiously" into his privacy, and interpreted his familiarity as the mark of one craving affection. Eglinton explains Moore's writing of *Hail and Farewell* as an Irish adventure undertaken as compensation for his disappointments in the Irish Renaissance. Having been turned away by Hyde, Yeats, and Lady Gregory as an impractical ally, he had determined to exact from them "a recompense which they had not bargained for."[51] Eglinton commended Moore for his common sense. The feeling was mutual. Moore refers to himself and Eglinton as "two old cronies."[52]

Hyde's lack of confidence in Moore as an ally in the work

of the Gaelic League was paid off by Moore with the accusation that Hyde was currying favor with all classes,—"members of Parliament, priests, farmers, shopkeepers," and that "by standing well with these people, especially with the priests" he had become the "arch-type of the Catholic-Protestant, cunning, subtle, cajoling, superficial and affable." It was by these qualities, Moore said, that Hyde had been able "to paddle the old dug-out of the Gaelic League up from the marshes." As for Hyde's own speech, Moore called it "the vilest English ever moulded by the lips of men."[53]

Moore admired A. E., was jealous of Lady Gregory, quarreled with Yeats, and called John Eglinton an "old crony." But the person with whom he was most continuously associated was his cousin Edward Martyn. Yeats said that they were "inseparable friends bound one to the other by mutual contempt."[54] He called them "the peasant sinner" and "the peasant saint."[55]

As is well known, Martyn was the constant butt of Moore's jokes. All the smallness of Moore's nature is revealed in the pains he took to set down in print all his petty triumphs over Martyn. He even set himself up as knowing more about music than Edward Martyn, and mocked him for referring to the *Adeste Fidelis* as plain chant and for mistaking the voice of a fifty-year old woman in a Paris choir for that of a boy.[56] Moore's attitude toward Martyn is too well known to need further documentation, but little attention has been paid to Martyn's reactions. Denis Gwynn has brought to light Martyn's previously unpublished *Paragraphs for the Perverse*. The conclusion of Martyn's paragraph on *Mon Ami Moore* justifies Joseph Hone's designation of the friendship as "familiar and grotesque":[57]

I am even stimulated by the perversity of that Donnybrook Fair type of Irishman, Mr. George Augustus Moore, who by constituting himself my Boswell has, like his prototype, obtained a notoriety of mean vanity, if not for the unique fidelity of the portraiture, an immortality which assuredly none of his other marks could bring him. *Mon ami Moore* yearns to be *le génie de l'amitié,* but unfortunately he can never be looked upon as a friend. For he suffers from an incurable com-

plaint which manifests itself in the form of a catarrh or loose-
ness of the brain which causes a perennial condition of mental
diarrhea. This must be shot somewhere at once, and necessarily over those nearest to him, his friends. Then, in order to
hide his infirmity, he pretends he has done something very
clever, and like the infant Morgante, when he misbehaves
himself, clapping his little hands he laughingly shouts: "I did
this because I knew I would annoy you." But it does not annoy somehow, I suppose because it is *mon ami Moore*.[58]

Considering the evidence against Moore as to his human
relationships, it is with mixed feelings that one reads his own
self-depreciatory comment: "For it is difficult for me to believe any good of myself. Within the oftentimes bombastic
and truculent appearance that I present to the world, trem-
bles a heart shy as a wren in the hedgerow or a mouse along
the wainscoting."[59]

Much more elusive are the records of the relationships of
James Joyce with other members of the modern Irish school.
John Eglinton recognized the stature of Joyce and in his *Irish
Literary Portraits* he has set down some slender accounts of
the attitude of Yeats and Lady Gregory toward Joyce. He
quotes Yeats as having said of the youthful Joyce, "Never have
I encountered so much pretension with so little to show for
it," and he makes the earliest of the references to the party
given by Lady Gregory to the literary intelligentsia of Dublin.
Joyce was not invited and, when told of the affair, he assured
his informer that he would attend. Eglinton admits that he
and his friends were uneasy. He said, "I can still see Joyce
with his air of half-timid effrontery, advancing toward his
unwilling hostess and turning away from her to watch the
company."[60]

Gogarty makes mention of the relationship between Lady
Gregory and Joyce in *As I Was Going down Sackville Street*:

Joyce knew better than I what was in the air, and what
was likely to be the future of the theatre in Ireland.
Who can measure how great was its loss when Lady Gregory gave him the cold shoulder . . . . After an unsuccessful
interview he met us in a "snug," where, very solemnly, with
his high well-stocked forehead bulging over his nose, he re-
cited solemnly, waving his finger slowly:

"There was a kind lady called Gregory
Said, 'Come to me poets in beggary!'
   But found her imprudence
   When thousands of students
Cried, 'All we are in that category'!"[61]

In *Ulysses* Joyce has Mulligan [Gogarty] accuse Stephen Dedalus [Joyce] of showing ingratitude by his unseemly references to Lady Gregory. Mulligan asks him why he cannot say something complimentary in the manner of Yeats, and he mocks Yeats for the amusement of the company:

> Longworth is awfully sick, he said, after what you wrote about that old hake Gregory. O you inquisitional drunken jew jesuit! She gets you a job on the paper and then you go and slate her drivel to Jaysus. Couldn't you do the Yeats touch?
> He went on and down, mopping, chanting with waving graceful arms:
> —The most beautiful book that has come out of our country in any time. One thinks of Homer.[62]

Perhaps Yeats deserved the thrust, for Colum reports Yeats as having said to the youthful Joyce, "I do not know whether you are a fountain or a cistern."[63] A story went the rounds of Dublin to the effect that Joyce had said to Yeats, "We have met too late; you are too old to be influenced by me." Colum makes mention of it in *The Road Round Ireland,* seemingly giving it credence. Later, in an article entitled "Oliver Gogarty on James Joyce," published in the *Saturday Review of Literature,* February 22, 1941, Colum said that the time had come to expunge from the record the alleged remark. He observed that the remark was "dramatically appropriate, but like many other dramatically appropriate remarks, it was never made." Colum's authority for the disclaimer was Joyce himself: "Joyce, who had the highest admiration for Yeats, who collaborated in an Italian translation of 'The Countess Cathleen,' assured me he never said anything of the kind."[64] The question remains: are we to believe Joyce?

It is a fact that during the first World War Yeats, Moore, and Edmund Gosse prevailed on Asquith to award a royal bounty of one hundred pounds to Joyce, who was living at the time in strained circumstances in Zurich.[65] It may be assumed, then, that the relationship between Yeats and Joyce grew to be one of mutual respect, though there was no personal association of the two.

There is evidence in *Ulysses* that, at least during the period of its composition, Joyce was not certain of the loyalty of Gogarty. John Eglinton has given a succinct analysis of their relationship which serves well as a preliminary view before examining Joyce's treatment of Gogarty in *Ulysses*. Eglinton wrote:

Chief among these friends was the incomparable "Buck Mulligan," Joyce's name for a now famous Dublin doctor—wit, poet, mocker, enthusiast, and, unlike most of his companions, blest with the means to gratify his caprices. He had a fancy for living in towers, and when I first heard of him, had the notion of establishing himself at the top of the Round Tower at Clondalkin; afterwards he rented from the Admiralty the Martello Tower at Sandycove, which presently became the resort of poets and revolutionaries . . . . Buck Mulligan's conversation, or rather his vehement and whimsical oratory, is reproduced with such exactness in *Ulysses* that one is driven to conclude that even then Joyce was taking notes.[66]

The first derogatory reference to Gogarty as Buck Mulligan in *Ulysses* is made by the father of Stephen Dedalus [Joyce] as Stephen's father was riding to the funeral of Paddy Dignam. Mr. Dedalus "snarled" to his companions: " 'He's in that lowdown crowd . . . . That Mulligan is a contaminated bloody doubledyed ruffian by all accounts. His name stinks all over Dublin . . . . A counter jumper's son.' "[67]

Near the end of the book Mr. Bloom warns Stephen against Mulligan: " 'I wouldn't personally repose much trust in that boon companion of yours who contributes the humorous element, Dr. Mulligan, as a guide, philosopher, and friend, if I were in your shoes. He knows which side his bread is buttered on though in all probability he never realised what it is to be without regular meals. Of course you didn't notice as much as I did but it wouldn't occasion me the least surprise to learn that a pinch of tobacco or some narcotic was put in your drink for some ulterior object.' "[68]

As Bloom continued, Stephen's face gave no indication one way or the other as to what he thought of the matter when Bloom gave him "a guarded glance of half solicitude."[69] Is this a new form of subtlety practiced by Joyce with the intention of warning the reader against confusing the opinion of Bloom with that of Bloom's creator? Be that as it may, one might infer as much from Bloom as he says:

> He understood, however, from all he heard, that Dr. Mulligan was a versatile allround man, by no means confined to medicine only, who was rapidly coming to the fore in his line and, if the report was verified, bade fair to enjoy a flourishing practice in the not too distant future as a *tony* medical practitioner drawing a handsome fee for his services in addition to which professional status his rescue of that man from drowning by artificial respiration . . . was . . . an exceedingly plucky deed which he could not too highly praise, so that he was utterly at a loss to fathom what earthly reason could be at the back of it except he put it down to sheer cussedness or jealousy, pure and simple.
> —Except it simply amounts to one thing and he is what they call picking your brains—[70]

Again, Bloom advises Stephen to "sever his connection with a certain budding practitioner, who, he noticed, was prone to disparage, and even, to a slight extent, with some hilarious pretext, when not present, deprecate him [Stephen] or whatever you like to call it, which, in Bloom's humble opinion, threw a nasty sidelight on that side of a person's character—no pun intended."[71]

Gogarty, in his turn, devotes part of a chapter in his memoirs to a chance meeting with Joyce in a public house. He records in connection with his account of the conversation that was carried on there that Joyce "sat on any resentment he bore by assuring himself that he would crucify us all in due course."[72]

With all this maze of accusation and recrimination at least one notable figure of the modern Irish school had little to do. While pages were being penned about the "aloofness" of Yeats, no irritation was being felt at the actual self-imposed isolation of John Millington Synge. Descriptions of the playwright have been drawn mentioning the self-absorption of the dreamer, but with no tinge of resentment. Yeats said that Synge "hardly seemed aware of the existence of other writers. I never knew if he cared for work of mine, but I do not remember that I had from him even a conventional compliment." According to Yeats, Synge was never "anxious to impress, or convince in any company." In fact, "Self-assertion was impossible to him."[73]

Lady Gregory said that the people of his plays were the real people among whom he lived and that his dreamy look came from this. She spoke of his spending a great deal of time wandering in the woods at Coole, where he was at home with the shy creatures of the wood and lake.[74]

L. A. G. Strong tells of Synge's appearance in the foyer of the Abbey Theatre after a performance where a large number of people were gathered: "With his back to the mantel Mr. Yeats addressed one knot of listeners; beneath the candelabra Lady Gregory addressed another. In a corner, having slipped behind a hat-stand to avoid attention was the third of the triumvirate, J. M. Synge."[75]

Gogarty contributes a similar picture:

In Camden Street, Synge would be sitting watching his rehearsals. He sat silent, holding his stick between his knees, his chin resting on his hands. He spoke seldom. When he did his talk came in a short rush, as if he wished to get the talk over as soon as possible. A dour, but not a forbidding man. Had he been less competent it might have been said of him on account of his self absorption that he "stood aloof from other minds. In impotence of fancied power." He never relaxed his mind from its burden.[76]

The man who, perhaps, knew Synge best was not Yeats, but, rather, Stephen MacKenna. E. R. Dodds has written of their association and of their common interests: "Synge and MacKenna made, in appearance, a strange pair, the one shy, silent, and morose, the other a born talker; but they had in common an ironic humour, a passionate interest in the problem of style, and an unresting curiosity about the secrets of religious experience."[77]

MacKenna affected the other members of the Dublin coterie variously. A. E. felt for him a deep regard which he acknowledged by dedicating *The Interpreters* to him, for the delight he had taken in MacKenna's translation of Plotinus. Dodds testifies to a certain liking between Eglinton and Mac-Kenna, who for a time lived in England only a few miles apart, although the two men differed in temperament and outlook. However, they had similar political views and both were in residence in England because they refused to give allegiance to the Irish Free State. Eglinton once took George Moore to visit MacKenna, but found the two men naturally antagonistic. MacKenna could see no value in the works of George Moore, and Moore looked with amusement on the clutter of musical instruments lying about MacKenna's rooms and "suspected him of being not much more than a picturesque charlatan."[78]

MacKenna once wrote to his brother Robert that he did not "care a button" about intellectual people, for they frightened and bored him. He made an exception in favor of James Stephens, whom he called the "simplest and friendliest soul alive" even though he was "eminent."[79]

A larger volume than this could be devoted to the whole maze of faction and concord. The main relationships may be briefly stated: Yeats counted as friends Lady Gregory, A. E., and Synge. A. E. got on well with all members of the group, although he occasionally quarreled lightly with Yeats and Moore. Synge was chary of giving himself up to any very close companionship, but seems to have been in close sympathy with MacKenna. Lady Gregory was hospitable and generous with all, however much her good will may have been abused in return, as it certainly was by mocking remarks made about her by Moore, Gogarty, Joyce, and Ervine. Moore's associations were all marred by a spirit of jealousy and by his undisciplined penchant for the reproof valiant and the reply churlish. Joyce bore for a time some resentment toward Lady

Gregory, but was not greatly affected by what she or any other member of the school thought of him. He came to admire the solid work of Yeats and held him in respect, an esteem which was reciprocated by Yeats when Joyce had reached maturity. Joyce did not declare openly his complete feeling for Gogarty, but by devoting so much attention to him in *Ulysses* as the character Buck Mulligan, he leaves no room to doubt that he appreciated Gogarty's intellect and keen wit. Eglinton, who seems to have kept his feelings under the control of reason, looked dispassionately upon the virtues and frailties of all his contemporaries among the Irish writers, even throwing out a good word for Moore now and then; he was one of the first to take the correct measure of James Joyce, who so early left Dublin to become a citizen of the world.

Relationships among other members of the school are less clearly defined. In general it may be said that nowhere has comment been more profusely personal than in the writings of the modern Irish, whose fiction and criticism are tinged with personal prejudice, and whose accusations and recriminations give zest to their letters and memoirs.

Chapter IX

LITERARY THEORIES AND UNDERLYING PHILOSOPHIES

An examination of the critical comment of the members of any school brings to light much that treats of literary theory and of the aesthetic and ethical philosophies underlying that theory. The gathering together of comment from both the organized and the random, or casual, criticism of the Irish writers themselves enables one to see how deliberate and self-conscious was the aesthetic of the modern Irish school and upon what bases it rests.

In order to find the central principles of the school it is well to determine first the basic concepts underlying the method of Yeats, who was the acknowledged leader of the school, and then to examine the critical support given those concepts by other members of the group. Each writer has, of course, put forth some subsidiary principles. Certain psychological factors, as well as the variation of the forms of expression elected by the individual members of the school, play a part in differentiating the methods of the various writers.

Artistic explorations of the mystic and the occult, and intellectual adventures in the realms of the arcane are fundamental to the subject matter of Yeats and fundamental to his method. His adaptation of the Symbolism of the French to the Celtic spirit was in harmony with that literary theory of his which placed an overwhelming emphasis on imagination as superior to reason.[1] In a letter to John O'Leary he once wrote: "The mystical life is the centre of all that I think and all that I write."[2]

At the core of his mysticism was his belief in "some great memory that renews the world and men's thoughts age after age."[3] Yeats believed that this great memory was the "dwelling house of symbols" and of "images that are living souls." The poet's subject matter derives from these symbols: "The poet of essences and pure ideas must seek in the half-lights that glimmer from symbol to symbol as if to the ends of the earth, all that the epic and dramatic poet finds of mystery and shadow in the accidental circumstance of life."[4]

A visionary concept of nature took precedence over factual observance of external display. John Eglinton was quick to perceive the direction in which this belief in poetry as a form of magic was leading Yeats. It was this theory of inspiration that caused him to become "less and less of what is called an open-air man," he said. "The enchanting poet of the *Lake Isle of Innisfree* and *The Man Who Dreamed of Fairyland* was still the enchanting poet of *The Embroidered Cloths* and of *The Fiddler of Dooney,* but his rhythms and imagery came to him more and more in visions of the night or from the ambiguous world of necromancy and séances."[5] George Moore observed the same early change in Yeats: ". . . before he met the Indian who had taught him metaphysics he used to take pleasure in the otter in the stream, the magpie in the hawthorn, and the heron in the marsh, the brown mice in and out of the corn-bin, and the ousel that had her nest in the willow under the brook."[6] Yeats acknowledges that his dissatisfaction with poetry that relied on descriptions of nature for the sake of nature directed him toward symbolism. "If people were to accept the theory that poetry moves us because of its symbolism, what change should we look for in the manner of our poetry?" he asked. And he fashioned the reply: "A return to the way of our fathers, a casting out of descriptions of nature for the sake of nature, of the moral law for the sake of the moral law, a casting out of all anecdotes and of that brooding over scientific opinion that so often extinguished the central flame in Tennyson."[7]

Although Yeats would cast out "the moral law, for the sake of the moral law," he did not underestimate the teaching power of literature. Writing of William Morris, he said, "Poets and artists have begun again to carry the burdens that priests and theologians took from them angrily some few hundred years ago."[8] Later, he wrote, conversely, this time while considering the work of Synge, "Only that which does not teach, which does not cry out, which does not persuade, which does not condescend, which does not explain, is irresistible."[9]

105

Again, after another lapse of time, he said in *Plays and Controversies* that he believed literature to be "the great teaching power of the world, the ultimate creator of all values."[10]

When one considers Yeats' attitude toward propaganda in relation to art, the seeming inconsistency falls into line. Yeats believed that the creation of an emotion of beauty was "the only kind of literature that justified itself . . . . Books of literary propaganda and literary history are merely preparations for the understanding of such an emotion."[11]

Yeats disliked writing which tended "to lose itself in externalities of all kinds, in opinion, in declamation."[12] He was getting close to the principle of "art for art's sake." In fact, he said that "literature differs from exploratory and scientific writing in being wrought about a mood, or a community of moods, as the body is wrought about an invisible soul."[13] And again, "The more a poet rids his verses of heterogeneous knowledge and irrelevant analysis and purifies his mind with elaborate art, the more does the little ritual of his verse resemble the great ritual of nature, and become mysterious and inscrutable."[14]

Yeats was constantly attacked for his personal aloofness among his associates. Aloofness of his expression was considered and intentional. It was his design to make his verse "mysterious and inscrutable." He said once in a letter to Katharine Tynan: "In the second part of 'Oisin' under disguise of symbolism I have said several things to which I only have the key. The romance is for my readers. They must not even know there is a symbol anywhere. They will not find out. If they did it would spoil the art, yet the whole poem is full of symbols—if it be full of aught but clouds."[15]

Yeats looked upon symbolism as of two sorts, traditional and personal: "There is indeed a systematic mystic in every poet or painter, who, like Rossetti, delights in traditional symbolism, or, like Wagner, delights in personal symbolism; and such men often fall into trances, or have waking dreams."[16] While Yeats looked upon this "curious indefinable symbolism" as "the substance of all style,"[17] he insisted that "art has never taken more than its symbols from anything that the eye can see or the hand measure"[18] and that poetry was derived from the poet's self: ". . . poetry and romance cannot be made by the most conscientious study of famous moments and of the thoughts and feeling of others, but only by looking into that little, infinite, faltering, eternal flame that we call ourselves."[19]

Yeats wrote to Dorothy Wellesley during the writing of the essays which were collected and printed under the title *On the Boiler*[20] and which have disappeared from the book markets, "My belief must go into what I write, even if I estrange friends; some when they see my meaning set out in plain print will hate me for poems which they have thought meant nothing."[21] Yeats reiterated numerous times his belief that "the imagination is the man himself and . . . the world as imagination sees it is the durable world."[22]

But the poet had a twofold personality, according to Yeats. His later philosophy developed the theory of the "antithetical self," or the "mask." Moreover, he looked upon all men as actors, all engaged in trying to become their opposites.[23] He said pointedly in this connection that "Synge was a sick man, picturing energy, a doomed man picturing gaiety"; that Lady Gregory, who was by nature proud and who lived by artifice, "was born to see the glory of the world in a peasant mirror," and that whereas he himself "ruffled in manly pose," he had, for all that, "a timid heart."[24] L. A. G. Strong says that although this doctrine was not a gift of Oscar Wilde, yet it was he who suggested it to Yeats by remarking that man could not speak the truth until he wore a mask.[25] A. E., in his essay *Song and Its Fountains,* writes that Yeats' preoccupation with his own myth of duality-in-self developed to its climax in the self-conscious expression in the *Vision,* "a gigantic philosophy of self and anti-self."[26]

Yeats had the curious notion, not uncommon to mystics, that by austerity of life or by ascetic practice he could purify his style and relieve it of all excess of ornament. In his autobiography he tells us that when fretting over what seemed to him the overelaborate style of *The Wanderings of Oisin* he had "thought for some weeks of sleeping upon a board."[27] Writing as an elderly man to Dorothy Wellesley, he spoke of emotional discipline and its resultant power: "We have all something within ourselves to batter down and get our power from this fighting. I have never 'produced' a play in verse without showing the actors that the passion of the verse comes from the fact that the speakers are holding down violence or madness—'down Hysterica passio.' All depends on the completeness of the holding down, on the striving of the beast underneath."[28] He continuously attempted to bring together "ecstasy, asceticism, and austerity," of which three Synge had said two often came together, but never three.[29] "The true poetic movement of our time," Yeats wrote, "is toward heroic discipline."[30] When he was gathering together poems for his edition of *The Oxford Book of Modern Verse* he rejected many poems about the first World War. He said in his preface to the anthology: "I have rejected these poems for the same reason that made Arnold withdraw his *Empedocles on Etna* from circulation; passive suffering is not a theme for poetry. In all the great tragedies, tragedy is a joy to the man who dies; in Greece the tragic chorus danced."[31]

The foregoing tenets are, in brief, the underlying philosophy of Yeats' craft. In practice he attempted to revive poetic drama, for he believed that the theatre was in need of reform and that poetic drama would revitalize the theatre. At the same time he felt urgently that the appreciation of verse, of the lyric specifically, could be revived among the people only by enabling the folk to hear verse chanted. Thus, by re-establishing poetic drama, Yeats hoped to serve two ends, to reform the theatre and to develop in the people an appreciation of verse. The theatre had fallen into a decadence by substituting "nervous tremors" for the "purification that comes with pity and terror to the imagination and intellect."[32] He expressed his dissatisfaction even more clearly: "The theatre grows more elaborate, developing the player at the expense of the poet, developing the scenery at the expense of the player, always increasing in importance whatever has come to it out of the mere mechanism of a building or the interests of a class, . . .

and creating a class before the footlights as behind, who are stirred to excitements that belong to it and not to life."[33]

In his labors for reform he set about trying to find "singers, minstrels and players who love words more than any other thing under heaven."[34] He told his fellow craftsmen that their writing for the theatre would increase their feeling for style. "Let us get back in everything to the spoken word."[35] He drew a distinction between the actor and the reciter, whose art was "always allusion, never illusion." One sees here his desire to revive the use of chorus and messenger: "The reciter must be made exciting and wonderful in himself" and will differ from his audience only in the exaltation of his mood.[36]

This leads one to a consideration of Yeats' theory of the audience as the inspiration of the poet-dramatist. "You must remember your audience," he said. "It is always there. You cannot write without it."[37] The audience should be primarily interested in the literary style and in the evocation of the spirit of beauty through symbolism. A self-improving and self-educating audience was a "perverted and commonplace audience."[38] Likewise the dramatist who prostituted his art to propaganda was to find no place in Yeats' reformed theatre. The word was all. "The theatre began in ritual," he wrote, "and it cannot come to its greatness again without recalling words to their ancient sovereignty."[39] This preoccupation with the sound of words has been described by L. A. G. Strong, who said: "He loved abracadabras and sounding names. They added a dignity to life, an impressiveness to speech. They were part of the technique of seeming, the more valuable because the mysteries behind them were real. They were as characteristic of him as the strange curved glasses in which he would offer wine to his friends, and one could believe that he chose his wines as much for their names as for their bouquet, rolling them on his tongue, and ending the recital 'and this is Itaalion vairmouth.' "[40]

Many of Yeats' extensive revisions were made in the search for the exact word though he was also given to rewriting in order to alter the structure of his stories, lyrics, and dramas. Revision was a constant literary practice of Yeats.

A line will take us hours maybe;
Yet if it does not seem a moment's thought,
Our stitching and unstitching has been naught.[41]

Lennox Robinson reminds the reader of his duty to judge *The Countess Cathleen* by its final version of 1912, but admits the interest one finds in tracing through its twenty years of mutation in versions from 1892, through 1895, and 1899 down to its final presentation.[42] Detailed studies have been made of the revision in Yeats' poetry and plays.[43] It suffices here to have called attention to his working method. He was a most deliberate artist.

It now remains to determine to what extent the associates of Yeats supported his views, which, for convenience, will be epitomized here as follows: the poet's function is to explore the realms of the abstract and to set down his perceptions of the truth, arrived at by the imagination, in the guise of symbols. These symbols are rooted in the literary and folk tradition and in the personality of the poet. The literary and folk symbols are readily grasped by the mind trained in the literary and folk traditions, but the personal symbol may or may not be understood by the reader. There is no obligation on the poet's part to unveil the meaning for the reader. The poet's subject matter is not made up of descriptions of external nature, nor in statements of moral law, nor in propaganda for political faith or religious creed, but rather of the expression of spiritual truths grasped by intuition and presented in metaphor. The expression, or style, is rooted in the poet's self, which is a duality—the real self striving towards its opposite, the visionary self. This striving creates a generative power which culminates in expression. The poet's inspiration derives from a disciplined austerity of life. His unceasing care is for the word. It is the business of the poet-dramatist to revive the value of the spoken word.

That Yeats felt A. E. to be in harmony with himself in the early years of their association is attested to by his dedication to A. E. of *The Secret Rose*: "Although I wrote these stories at different times and in different manners . . . they have but one subject, the war of spiritual with natural order; and how can I dedicate such a book to anyone but you, the one poet of Modern Ireland who has moulded a spiritual ecstasy into verse?"[44] In a letter to Katharine Tynan, Yeats referred to A. E. as "a mystic of medium type."[45] Both young men were meeting with the Dublin Theosophical Society and were studying Indian philosophy. A. E., in turn, commended Yeats as the first poet to disclose the "revelation of the spirit as the weaver of beauty" and as one who shadowed forth the "great mysteries in unnoticed things."[46]

For various reasons, some of which have been previously noted in this study, Yeats and A. E. drew apart, and, late in life, shortly before his death, A. E. wrote to Mrs. Kingsley Porter: "Yes, there was a time when Yeats called himself a symbolist and would have made me out to be one, but I preferred mysticism to symbolism . . . . However the meaning of words grows and all literature is symbolism in some fashion."[47] As a matter of fact, even in those early days, A. E. had written to Yeats, "Your detestable symbols too get a reflected light from the general twilight luminousness and beauty which does not belong to them by right, just as moonlight makes an ugly scene beautiful."[48]

A. E. made himself clear on the point of the relationship of the imagination and the intellect. Noting that L. A. G. Strong was dilating on a text which he had furnished when reviewing a book of poetry, a text which ran, "The poet knows that the imagination should be master and the intellect the slave in the house of the soul," A. E. felt that he should revise his statement. He had come to believe that "the intellect and the imagination should in the poet be one and indivisible, and if there is a dramatic sundering of these faculties, if the first be dominant there will be no poetry, and if the second be dominant there may be but little common sense . . . and this is but another way of affirming Rossetti's statement that there must be fundamental brain work in fine poetry."[49]

However, in spite of these departures, an examination of the work of both poets and of the judgments of the contemporary Irish critics will establish the fact that the two poets did not diverge widely in their fundamental concepts. Indeed, it was

A. E. who popularized the theory of the race memory as a source of poetic inspiration. A. E. felt that the fountains of song were dreams, waking dreams, the latter being in part ancestral memories connected with the pre-existence of the soul. Padraic Colum said that no other poet of Ireland was as cosmic as A. E. "Everything he knows, everything he feels, has a history that is before the stars and sun." A. E.'s notion of men as "strayed Heaven dwellers," Colum reminds us, not only runs through his poetry, but is also expressed in his pictures and economics.[50]

A. E. believed that the great scientist could also be a mystic, that he could "make the nicest and most minute investigations, mathematical or by delicate instruments, into the nature of matter and energy and yet give credit to the mystic and his intuitional method of discovering truth."[51] This mysticism of A. E. has been treated by every member of the Dublin school. Yeats said that "men watched him with awe or with bewilderment," for it was known that he saw visions continually.[52] Katharine Tynan describes his youthful practices: "He used sometimes to spend a night on the Dublin mountains, where he had revelations and met strange people. He was always perfectly sincere and perfectly simple, so that when he told you of some wonderful meeting you only felt that it must have happened somehow . . . . When he tells you in one of his incarnations he was a dishonest merchant of Bagdad, and has to cleanse himself from that stain through successive incarnations, you receive it as though you were in the Arabian Nights."[53] It is unnecessary to labor the point of A. E.'s faith in the mystic's power of discovering truth. There is plenty of evidence that his mysticism supports Yeats' theory of poetry as deriving from the "mystery of imagination" and from controlling images by giving them symbolic meaning:

How can we explain the mystery of imagination, the power we discover in ourselves which leaps upon us, becoming master of ideas, images and words, taking control of these from the reasoning mind, giving to them symbolic meanings, until images, ideas and words, swept together, become an intellectual organism by some transcendental power superior to all reasoning? It is as mysterious as the growth of an organism in nature which draws from earth by some alchemy the essences it transmutes and makes subservient to itself.[54]

A. E. saw the mystic and the seer in other members of the Dublin group. Of Stephen MacKenna he wrote: "We surmise what agonies of literary conscience went into the choice of words so that they might convey not merely intellectual meaning, but that we might ourselves fly into that spiritual aether and feel the ecstasy of the seer and tremble as he does with the beauty of his vision."[55] He was constantly looking for this spiritual kinship among his associates, saying that "even Stephens and Colum, who write so often of what the eye sees, write most often as if it were remembered in dream or reverie."[56] He said later that the "psychic energy" in Stephens' poetry was the quality which he most esteemed in that poetry. Stephens' stories, he said, were symbols for things in the imagination.[57] He justified Yeats' later poetry because of its "intellectual adventures into . . . mysticism and symbolism, into magic and spiritualism and many ways of thought which most people regard as by-ways that lead no whither."[58] He felt that there was no writer in the history of literature "more purely and inhumanly exotic" than Dunsany.[59]

This sense of accord was not one-sided. James Stephens said himself that there probably never was an intellectual artist and that there probably never would be one, "for life is being, and the artistic reaction is an emotional one."[60] Lord Dunsany, in his memoirs, described the mystic voice which speaks to the poet, with the implication that the experience had been his own:

> . . . at moments unknown, always unexpected, there comes that clear voice in his mind, and with a feeling surely of ignorance and of awe he finds himself speaking of cities he has known and byways he has trod in lands where the desert has long since covered all, coming back again to its own, where the historian can only guess and the traveller durst not go. He speaks of things that were before cities began, and of gods that walked with him in the prime of the stars. The voice passes . . . and he is only a man again, with a man's humiliations.[61]

George Moore considered the mysticism of Yeats and A. E. as the predominant phase of their characters which he molded into one in the person of Ulick Dean in his novel, *Evelyn Innes.*[62] There is no hint here that George Moore was out of sympathy with their occult interests. Moreover, did not George Moore assign his return to Ireland to the influence of that voice he heard calling him as he was walking near the Strand?

The symbolic nature of the writings of James Joyce was recognized by other Irish writers. Yeats wrote to Katharine Tynan Hinkson in April, 1914: "I have been sending people to your 'Wild Harp' [an anthology] to read that last poem of Joyce—that curious symbolic thing."[63] Later in *Wheels and Butterflies,* he spoke of *Ulysses* as suggestive of "a philosophy like that of the Samkara school of ancient India."[64] There is much of Yeats' and A. E.'s theory of the trance in Joyce's theory of the "Epiphany," as he called it, wherein the artist arrives at a temporary obliviousness of everything in his environment save one sole object, or facet of a situation, which becomes so revealed, as if with magic light, that the artist is able to see and recognize the essence of the thing in the flash of an instant's duration. He sees into the life of things by an intuitive power exercised as if by some force outside his own will.[65] The mystic seldom makes claim for more. This is what John Eglinton referred to as the "abnormal power of spiritualized egoism."[66] The fact that *Ulysses* is a master work of symbolism in union with naturalism is too obvious to require proof here.

One may fairly conclude that a strain of acknowledged mysticism expressing itself symbolically runs through many of the writers of the modern Irish school. Their minds were filled with fantasy and they yearned for mystic experience.

The emphasis on the personality of the poet is likewise found in the critical writings of and about A. E., Synge, Colum, Stephens, and Joyce. "It is of more importance to us," said A. E., "to have experience than to have philosophies."[67] He was more emphatic when he wrote that "the slightest personal experience of the spirit is worth *as poetry* more than all the greatest teachers, repeated with no matter how much reverence."[68] Colum quotes Sygne as saying that all his work was subjective and derived from his own moods in his own life. He calls attention to the "sombre personal feeling" from which Sygne derived his *Riders to the Sea*: "*Riders to the Sea* had come out of the feeling that old age was coming upon him—he was not forty at the time—and that death was making approach. And it is this sombre personal feeling that makes the play."[69] This seeing life subjectively had obscured Synge's view because his "unrealized personality" was in a state of chaos, according to L. A. G. Strong, who felt that Synge achieved distinction finally only because his life on Aran had taught him to turn his gaze outward.[70] On the other hand, Darrell Figgis thought that the Aran experience had liberated the personal philosophy of the man: "That he should have spoken of himself on a crucial event near the end of his days as reading Spinoza is significant; but philosophies do not make a man; a man weaves his philosophy from his temperament, or loves that philosophy to which his soul inclines. Self is itself; and the September night on Aran Island was before Spinoza."[71] James Stephens said that the artist was "always engaged upon his own portrait," and that not merely his choice of subject, but also his management of it, was a "definite statement about himself."[72] Stephen Dedalus, in conversation with Eglinton, Best, and others of the Dublin literati, reflected that "every life is many days, day after day. We walk through ourselves, meeting robbers, ghosts, giants, old men, young men, wives, widows, brother-in-love. But always meeting ourselves."[73] In *A Portrait of the Artist as a Young Man* Joyce had previously written: "The personality of the artist passes into the narration itself, flowing round and round the persons and the action like a vital sea."[74]

However trite the idea may be that the poet's expression is rooted in his personality, the Irish writers nevertheless made personal avowals of their faith in the idea.

Yeats' theory of the "mask" or the dual nature of the personality, was not exploited by other members of the school. However, ideas which E. R. Dodds says remain close to the core of Stephen MacKenna's thinking have much in common with Yeats' theory. As revealed by Dodds, MacKenna said in an unpublished commonplace book:

Behind and above the thinking and feeling and willing soul,

or souls, is the real Man—the unalloyed soul, which studies and judges the others. It does not so much feel as see that the inferior souls of him, the outer husk of the spirit, feels. This is the calm lonely thing, really untroubled by the vagaries of life, which presides over all . . . . Its pronouncement is immutable: it is all that the Man will ever see of truth; it is the unquestionable fruit of his individuality; it is his entire draft upon the 'All Knowledge' . . . . It is the Dweller in the threshold, looking before and after, seeing things material and things spiritual in their whole nature and tendency—but always by its own light . . . . Here is the ground of the Equality of Man—and of certain equality in all nature . . . . The criminal is often a moral idiot, essentially undefiled: often one feels in dealing with those whose conduct one most abhors that it is only the outer husk of one's own soul that is disgusted and repelled and only by the outer husk of their soul. It is why we may often love a person without caring to say we respect him.

Dodds remarks that such a conception of man involves a corresponding view of art, which, in fact, MacKenna did briefly state: "The art of expression in poetry and in philosophy is the art of descent: it is limiting and cabining the wide vision of the spirit: it is telling a truth so as to be understood, not so as to be true; it is materialising the spiritual and losing much in the decanting."

Dodds knew that these thoughts were far from new in 1897. "But," he said, "there is something in the young man's statement of them which suggests that for him they were not so much the fruit of reading as the expression of a temperament and of an inner experience."[75]

As for the writer's lack of a sense of obligation to make himself intelligible to the reader, one sees how far the spirit of Yeats could travel in that matter when one attempts to read Joyce's *Finnegans Wake.* It is certainly clear that Yeats and Joyce were of one mind on that point, though Yeats' obstacles are of little consequence in comparison with those set up by Joyce. Yeats' associates, however, were not expressive on this detail.

There was general agreement among the Irish writers on the question of the elimination of propaganda and of the poet's mission as teacher. George Moore, in the preface to his *Anthol-*

ogy of Pure Poetry, which amounts to a defense of "art for art's sake," remarks that "Shakespeare never soiled his songs with thought"[76] and that he himself was "whole-heartedly for Ulalume."[77] "The world is littered with dead literature as with leaves."[78] He is explicit in assigning the cause to propaganda: "Every ten years morality, patriotism, duty and religion, take on meanings different from those they wore before, and that is why each generation, dissatisfied with the literature that preceded it, is inspired to write another literature round the new morality, the new patriotism, the new duty, the new religion, a literature which seems to the writers more permanent than the literature their fathers wrote, but which is destined to pass away as silently."[79] His avowal is even more clearly expressed in *Hail and Farewell:* "All conventions of politics, society, and creed, yes, and of Art, too, must be cast into the melting pot; he who would be an artist must melt down all things; he must discover new formulas, new moulds, all the old values must be swept aside, and he must arrive at a new estimate. The artist should keep himself free from all creed, from all dogma, from all opinion. As he accepts the opinions of others he loses his talent, all his feelings and his ideas must be his own, for Art is a personal re-thinking of life from end to end, and for this reason the artist is always eccentric."[80]

Synge is in agreement with Yeats and Moore. In his preface to *The Tinker's Wedding,* he declares that the drama does not teach or prove anything: "Analysts with their problems and teachers with their systems, are soon as old-fashioned as the pharmacopoeia of Galen .... The best plays of Ben Jonson and Molière can no more go out of fashion than the blackberries on the hedges."[81] The third of that dramatic triad, Lady Gregory, gives us the printed form sent out with manuscripts rejected by the Abbey: "We do not desire propagandist plays, nor plays written mainly to serve some obvious moral purpose; for art seldom concerns itself with those interests or opinions that can be defended by argument, but with realities of emotion and character that become self-evident when made vivid to the imagination."[82]

Yeats spoke rather condescendingly of Padraic Colum as

"too young to be content with laughter," but, because of his youth, excused his interest in the reform of society, and expressed a hope that he would come to see that the only reality is within the mind.[83] But L. A. G. Strong compares Colum to Blake and speaks of his intuitive wisdom.[84]

John Eglinton, in reviewing Yeats' *The Tower*, compared pure poetry to music which moves to a faith in immortality merely by its emotional content. "It is when poetry subsists wholly within itself,"he said, "tending thus to the condition of music, that it is most persuasive." He did not believe that poetry could subsist without thought, but he felt that that was a different thing from making assertions.[85] This was unquestionably the view of Yeats.

Yeats' attitude toward poetic description of nature for the sake of nature was shared by A. E. and Synge, Stephens, and Gogarty. George Moore tells us that A. E. was insistent upon keeping descriptions of nature out of the play *Diarmuid and Grania,* on which they were collaborating. A. E. said that such references to nature as were made "should be drawn from a general knowledge of nature rather than from any particular observation of a particular place."[86] Critics frequently remarked upon Synge's ability to evoke a scene in nature by a few suggestive words rather than by specific description.[87]

Perhaps the doctrine of austerity, of plain living and high thinking, was bred in many of the Irish writers by the circumstances of their early youth, as for example in James Stephens and James Joyce. It is more likely, however, that Yeats and A. E. and John Eglinton were inspired by the Brahman philosophy. The remarks of Eglinton contain a pertinent analysis of the point:

Any acquaintance with the doctrines of Brahmanism and Buddhism suggests that mankind might have developed along other lines than have been chosen by the Western races. We have achieved to some extent the scientific conquest of Nature, but power over nature might conceivably have been achieved in some other way, and the tradition has always existed, and is far too widely diffused to be ignored, that by the practice of austerities and of intense concentration faculties may be developed, in the first place of complete self-control, and next, of control over nature, wherever Nature limits or obstructs the ascendant spirit of man.[88]

A. E., in reviewing Yeats' *A Packet for Ezra Pound,* said that he thought the poet should exercise himself in some hard intellectual labor after writing a book of poetry before he should begin to supplicate the Muse again.[89] But his philosophy made no exorbitant demands upon man's nature. He held the reasonable view that "almost all rich natures retain the power of playing at times, that is, of enjoying life without torturing themselves all the while about the wisdom or folly of what they are doing, just as the kitten enjoys chasing its own tail."[90] Frank O'Connor, whose tone frequently carries a slur upon Yeats, called Yeats "a propagandist" who was "much less a nationalist than an ascetic who asks his fellow writers to take a vow of poverty."[91]

Just how far Yeats' associates were willing to go in the matter of sacrifice of the flesh to the spirit is hard to determine by direct reference, but certainly the impressions gathered from general accounts do not lead one to believe that George Moore, Lord Dunsany, or Oliver Gogarty felt any urge toward asceticism.

Earlier chapters of this study have indicated the degree of support Yeats received in his adventures in the drama. It was pointed out that Edward Martyn withdrew from the theatre movement largely because he had no interest in the peasant play. George Moore's genius drew him to the novel as a form of expression. And finally, Synge broke the mold of Irish drama as Yeats had conceived it and turned it into new channels. Drama at the Abbey Theatre became less remote, less idealistic, and certainly less poetic than Yeats had hoped. But all the writers of the Irish school were agreed upon one point at least. The stage was in need of reform. Many expressions of recognition of this need are to be found among Yeats' associates. Lord Dunsany said that the London stage lured authors to "begin at the wrong end and write stagey things and things that will suit certain popular actors" and that, as an afterthought, the playwright would turn to the Muse of Tragedy and say, "and of course you will come too, my dear."[92] Lady Gregory, who said that the "de-

sire to experiment" was "like fire in the blood,"[93] has left a
rich record of the part she played in theatre reform, in *Our Irish
Theatre*. She was sufficiently in accord with Yeats to work har-
moniously with him over a long period of time, collaborating
in both writing and directing plays.

St. John Ervine was caustic in his criticism of Yeats' theories
of acting:

> He was then interested in the more esoteric forms of drama,
> and was eager to put masks on the actors' faces.[94] He wished to
> eliminate the personality of the player from the play . . . . There
> was some inconsistency in his talk about acting: at one moment
> he was anxious for anonymous, masked players, "freed" from
> personality, and at the next moment, he was demanding that
> players should act with their entire bodies, not merely with
> their voices and faces . . . . It is, perhaps, unfair to treat a man's
> "table-talk" as if it were a serious proposal . . . but so much of
> Mr. Yeats' talk and writing is related to this matter of disem-
> bodiment and passionless action, that it is difficult not to treat
> it seriously. For my part, I have always been unable to under-
> stand how it is possible for a human being to behave as if he
> were not a human being.[95]

L. A. G. Strong was sympathetic with Yeats' feeling for the
poetic drama, but he cautioned the playwright that stage presentation required something more than mere poetry: "There
is a great place and a great need for poetry on the stage: *but it
must be poetry the value of which is enhanced by stage presentation*. It must give the stage something, and the stage must give
it something."[96]

John Eglinton, ever the disinterested bystander and the re-
liable critic, observed that Yeats had found his solution to his
dramatic problems in the Noh-plays of Japan. His solution was
thanklessly received in the Abbey Theatre, said Eglinton,[97] and
one may rely on the accuracy of Eglinton's observation. But the
great thing is this: Yeats gave his unlimited support to Synge
when that dramatic genius was under fire, and publicly demonstrated a willingness to yield precedence to one who may have
been a greater dramatist, but who was certainly not a greater
poet. With this leadership, others rallied to the support of

Synge, and the homogeneity of the Dublin coterie remained the paramount force.

The Irish writers were completely in accord in their instinctive feeling for speech. It was Yeats' intention to exalt the poetic word. Practically every Irish writer has left an account of his own preoccupation with the sounds of words. It is not to be wondered at that words should have become for Joyce "his ritual, his incantation" or that he should have been "as serious in their use as any priest."[98] Who does not recall the attention given to sounds by the schoolboy, Stephen Dedalus? "And from here and there came the sounds of the cricket bats through the soft grey air. They said: pick, pack, pock, puck: little drops of water in a fountain slowly falling in the brimming bowl."[99] Joyce returns again and again in that early study, *A Portrait of the Artist as a Young Man,* to a consideration of language. His imagination plays like sheet lightning over his memories. Joyce said that he could not speak or write the words "home," "Christ," or "Master" "without unrest of spirit."[100]

John Eglinton contemplates Joyce's word juggling and arrives at a conclusion as original as ironic. This word-play was, he said, Joyce's Celtic revenge on the English:

> . . . It must have seemed to him that he held English, his country's spiritual enemy, in the hollow of his hand, for the English language too came at his call to do his bidding. This language found itself constrained by its new master to perform tasks to which it was unaccustomed in the service of pure literature; against the grain it was forced to reproduce Joyce's fantasies, in all kinds of juxtapositions, neologisms, amalgamations, truncations, words that are only found scrawled up in public lavatories, obsolete words, words in limbo or belike in the womb of time. It assumed every intonation and locution of Dublin, London, Glasgow, New York, Johannesburg. Like a devil taking pleasure in forcing a virgin to speak obscenely, so Joyce rejoiced darkly in causing the language of Milton and Wordsworth to utter all but unimaginable filth and treason.
>
> Such is Joyce's Celtic revenge.[101]

Dunsany's preoccupation with the sound of words led him in a different direction, but he, too, was conscious of this joy in the syllable:

And now my head began to fill with the sounds of Greek and Latin words, and continued to do so afterwards at Eton, until my memory held the echoes of more stately syllables than I knew the meanings of, and, when geography was tumbled on top of this, my mind was very full of the material needed for the names of strange rivers and cities. And these, when I came to write, my mind put together for itself; and, on the rare occasions when it has failed to do so and I have used conscious effort instead the name has always been uninteresting, unconvincing . . . . [102]

It is only the attraction of the word that compels attention, Dunsany said: " . . . if a man starts his story with such words as At Padan Aram in the field of Luz, the ears of the world will be turned to him. While words of the profoundest import, plodding their way barefooted without that chariot called Rhythm, scarce come within sight of the ardours that dwell in the reason of man."[103]

Eglinton remarks upon Moore's sense of language and diction. He once pleased Moore by saying that "to use a cliché with distinction was the mark of a good style." Moore's monotony, said Eglinton, was due to uniformity of sentence structure and certain pet mannerisms, but his love for "the proved and genuine usages of the English speech" was "as if he had been their father."[104]

The glamour of the word enticed Synge and MacKenna also. According to Colum, Synge "used to say that words had a cycle of life; the time came when they were too worn out for journalism even." Eventually the word might be taken up again and filled with dramatic import. Colum recorded MacKenna's discussion of the "contrasts in the genius of language":

He went on to talk of contrasts in the genius of languages, and gave lists of place names to illustrate them. I remember now only one contrasted pair, Verona and Ennis Kerry: both beautiful names, but one like a rich fabric and the other, he said, like a coloured rag caught on a hedge—for a coloured rag caught on a hedge is beautiful. Then he talked about the Greek and Gaelic words for the moon: both meant "the shiner" and could be contrasted with the English or French names which are expressive of glamour and beaminess. He could speak memorably upon such themes.[105]

A. E. and Yeats carried on their discussion of *the word* in letters extending from 1900 to 1936. A. E. was fearful of the hypnotic power of the word and contended for the current of idea which inspired the word. In 1900 he wrote to Yeats: ". . . Ideas have a beauty in themselves apart from words, and in literature or art I think the aim of the writer should be to afford an avenue to the idea, and make the reader forget the words or painting or sound which first evoked it."[106] He remained consistent. In 1936 he said again that he did not believe at all in "the power of words to convince apart from the current that inspired them."[107]

The Irish writer may have stood in need of some such caution as A. E.'s, for there is no denying that the Irish writer of the modern school is typical of his race[108]—a people distinguished for fluency in speech and aptness in metaphor—and sometimes subject to pitfalls by following the word as a will-o'-the-wisp.

A school of writers holding so much literary theory in common as did the members of the modern Irish school might be expected to collaborate with one another in order to strengthen that theory and might also be expected to exert mutual influences beyond actual collaboration. Such was, indeed, the case, and the critical comment upon these relationships may now be examined.

Chapter X
COLLABORATIONS AND INFLUENCES

Several members of the Dublin School undertook at various times to collaborate with one another, chiefly in the production of plays. The collaborators have in every instance left elaborate accounts of their proceedings and have also made acknowledgments of influences from within the group which have altered the individual character and style of specific works. The critics who were not personally involved in the collaborations have also made frequent comment upon these various projects and upon the mutual influences within the group. An examination of all the acknowledgments and observations clarifies yet further the interrelationships among the modern Irish writers.

Some of these efforts at collaboration were happy in their results, but occasionally the attempts ended in ill feeling between the collaborators. Among the former may be instanced the association of Lady Gregory and Yeats, although there is not perfect unanimity among critics in estimating the value of the collaboration. For instance, Lennox Robinson believes that Yeats would have developed better characters had he been left to himself, and refers to Yeats' *The Player Queen* and to the old man in *The Death of Cuchulain* as "entirely satisfactory" inventions realized without the assistance or influence of Lady Gregory.[1] The view that Lady Gregory's influence was not beneficial is likewise held by Padraic Colum, who, in reviewing Yeats' *Plays in Prose and Verse* in *The Yale Review* of January, 1925, indicates that *Cathleen ni Houlihan* and *The Pot of Broth* are by virtue of the fact that they were subjected to even remote collaboration with Lady Gregory not quite typical of Yeats' mind. "The last play in the volume, 'The Player Queen,'" Colum writes, "is really the typical Yeats play, in spite of the fact that it is the only play he has written the scene of which is not laid in Ireland and the fable of which is not based on Irish tradition."[2]

It seems rather odd that all editions of the plays written jointly by Yeats and Lady Gregory which appeared before her death in 1932 carried lengthy acknowledgments by Yeats of Lady Gregory's assistance, but that the two subsequent editions, with one slight exception, have dropped such prefatory comment. The circumstance suggests that the acknowledgments may have been overgenerous, and may have been made primarily through a sense of indebtedness for favors other than those strictly literary, such as Lady Gregory's liberal hospitality continuously offered at Coole and her generosity in lending considerable sums of money during those periods when Yeats' worldly fortunes were at a low ebb. On the other hand, he may have preferred eventually to gather all the credit to himself.

Among the dedicatory appreciations, that of Yeats, prefatory to *Plays for an Irish Theatre,* is the most detailed and significant. It takes the form of a letter which begins: "My dear Lady Gregory, I dedicate to you two volumes of plays that are in part your own." He then tells her of how he used to wander about Rosses Point as a boy, listening to the old stories and songs, and of how he brought them together in *The Celtic Twilight.* He speaks of the disrupting influence of life in London and of how Lady Gregory had, upon his return to Ireland, brought him again into contact with the cottagers. "You taught me to understand again, and much more perfectly than before, the true countenance of country life," he wrote. He then speaks of the difficulty he had had in reflecting the speech of the people in the speech of the characters in *Cathleen ni Houlihan.* And, finally, he writes: "We turned my dream into the little play . . . and when we gave it to the little theatre in Dublin and found that the working people liked it, you helped me put my other dramatic fables into speech."[3]

Yeats reprinted this preface of 1903 in his notes to *Plays in Prose and Verse,* in 1928. Thus he was continuing his acknowledgments a quarter of a century after their initial printing. To the reprint he adds the significant statement that among all the plays in the collection only *The Green Helmet* and *The Player Queen* are wholly his. Moreover, he declares *The Unicorn from the Stars* but for character and fable to be wholly Lady Gregory's work.[4] That is, the actual writing of the dialogue is altogether her work. Since the plays in this edition included, besides the three plays already mentioned, *Cathleen ni Houlihan, The Pot of Broth,*[5] *The Hour Glass, The King's Threshold, On Bailie's Strand, The Shadowy Waters,* and *Deirdre,* we may believe that Lady Gregory had a large part in the writing of eight of these plays which are usually associated only with the name of Yeats, and that Yeats actually wrote only two of the plays alone. Yeats says even more specifically in a letter to Lady Wellesley that Lady Gregory wrote the end of his *Deirdre.*[6]

In the preface to *The Unicorn from the Stars* published in 1908, Yeats tells the reader that Lady Gregory had refused to sign any of the plays other than the one which gives the volume its name. Yeats says that his share in that play consisted chiefly in the idea that "the rough life of the road and the frenzy of the poet" could be embodied in one character.[7] Lady Gregory's name, however, precedes that of her co-author, Yeats. In the 1934 edition of the *Collected Plays of Yeats* her name is dropped from the title-page, and there is a subtle difference in the text of the prefatory acknowledgment: "I have explained my indebtedness to Lady Gregory. If I could have persuaded her she would have signed *The Unicorn from the Stars,* her share in it is so great. She had generally some part wherever there is dialect, and often where there is not."[8]

What of the other eight plays? The *Collected Plays* carries no acknowledgment of Lady Gregory's part in them.

Perhaps it will never be known what modicum of idea in *The Unicorn from the Stars* was contributed by George Moore, although it is an acknowledged fact that the play is the revamping of a play called *Where There is Nothing,* which was whipped up in great haste by Yeats and Lady Gregory to preserve the theme from being plagiarized by George Moore. Yeats gives his version of Moore's connection with the play, in his autobiography. He says that he had outlined the plot of the play to Moore and had asked for his collaboration. Before such a procedure could get under way, Moore had fallen out with the director of the Irish Literary Theatre and had withdrawn from the theatre movement. Yeats, then, had written Moore that he felt himself obliged to go ahead with the play alone. A few weeks later Moore telegraphed Yeats that he had written a novel "on that scenario we composed together" and threatened to get an injunction if Yeats used the plot. Yeats replied, also by telegraph, that he would use nothing of Moore's but would certainly use his own plot. Whereupon he elicited the aid of Lady Gregory and of another person, "a cautious friend" whose anonymity has been preserved, and who, together with Yeats, wrote the five-act tragedy, *Where There is Nothing,* and published it as a supplement to *The United Irishman.* Yeats had called Moore's bluff. There is not the slightest evidence that Moore had written the announced novel. But the action taken by Yeats so promptly was felt by Moore as an injury, or personal affront, and relations between the two men were never cordial thereafter. Yeats expresses regret at his own precipitancy: "I look back with some remorse. Had I abandoned my plot and made him write the novel, he might have put beside *Muslin* and *The Lake* a third masterpiece, but I was young, vain and self-righteous and bent on proving myself a man of action. *Where There is Nothing* is a bad play .... In later years, with Lady Gregory's help I turned it into *The Unicorn from the Stars.*"9 Yeats makes other references to this affair, as, for example, in his notes to *Plays in Prose and Verse,* where he speaks of the great speed with which *Where There is Nothing* was produced "to meet a sudden emergency." He says that the five acts were written in a fortnight.10

N. J. O'Connor attributes the symbolism of *The Unicorn from the Stars,* which was the rewritten *Where There is Nothing,* to Yeats, and the characterization of the country folk to Lady Gregory.11

Lady Gregory's accounts of her collaboration with Yeats do not differ materially from those of Yeats. She adds a note, now and then, as for example, her reference to her play, *The Travelling Man:* "Neither Mr. Yeats nor I take the writing of our plays lightly. We work hard to get clearly both fable and idea. *The Travelling Man* was first my idea and then we wrote it together. Then Mr. Yeats wrote a variant of it as a Pagan play, *The Black Horse,* and to this we owe the song 'There's many a strong farmer whose heart would break in two.' It did not please him, however, and then I worked it out in my own way."[12]

Gogarty, in his customary manner of belittling Lady Gregory, suggests that probably she owed more to Yeats for the ideas in her plays than is generally recognized. In his reminiscences of Dublin, Gogarty pictures himself as sitting in the theatre without a program; it occurs to him that a program is not necessary, since one of Lady Gregory's "namby-pamby" plays is sure to be on the bill. As he is about to leave the theatre in order to escape anything so deadening to his spirits, the question arises in his mind:

> How much of her plays did she write? Yeats had spent many months annually in collaboration with her in Coole Park, and I knew how generously Yeats presented me, for one, with golden lines or ideas . . . .
> I almost got him to acknowledge his authorship of "The Rising of the Moon." I think he said that it was understood between himself and Lady Gregory that a play might be attributed to the one who had had the idea!
> Possibly Lady Gregory thought of the title, which was that of a well known ballad.[13]

This attitude of Gogarty and similar views of others among the Dublin school must have been known to Lady Gregory and may have prompted her expression of the hope that someone would throw a kind word after her because of her encouragement of Yeats. She testified as to her fostering care, declaring that his volume, *The Wind among the Reeds,* would never have been finished if she had not invited him to Coole.[14] Yeats was not niggardly of that kind word and said in his autobiography that he doubted if he should have done much with his life had it not been for "her firmness and her care."[15]

Except for an occasional contemptuous reference here and there, the associates of Yeats and Lady Gregory presented their harmony as natural and unforced. Out of their mutual respect and sympathy there developed the practice of literary collaboration productive of plays of merit. Whether each would have done better individually may be arguable. The fact is this: there was collaboration and the result was playable drama.

Yeats and Lady Gregory together provided a scenario for Dr. Hyde's *The Nativity.* Lady Gregory alone provided the scenario for Hyde's plays, *The Marriage* and *The Poorhouse.*[16] Hyde was further indebted to Yeats for the theme of *The Twisting of the Rope.* That little one-act comedy in Gaelic is based upon the story of Red Hanrahan in Yeats' *The Secret Rose.* Stephen Gwynn compares the two works: "The Hanrahan of Mr. Yeats is a man who has worked magic, and raised a fairy lover, and incurred her wrath, and is therefore under a curse, who moves through the world like a creature in a dream. The Hanrahan of Dr. Hyde's play is a creature more solidly established on the earth; ... easily to be persuaded once he has drink taken, that he is king of all Ireland."[17] Gwynn rates the comedy higher than Yeats' story.

Yeats' collaboration with Moore was fraught with difficulty.[18] Had the two men listened to Lady Gregory they would have spared themselves many a bitter quarrel over matters of style and structure. She had urged Moore to drop the matter of collaborating with Yeats on the play *Diarmuid and Grania* because she disliked to see Yeats' attention drawn from the writing of poems.[19] She argued that no good could derive from a man of genius and a man of talent coming together,[20] and Moore, recognizing whom she designated as the man of genius, could retaliate in no better way than by insisting on continuing in the attempt to write a play with Yeats.

The circumstances surrounding this attempt are rather well known, having been detailed by both parties in their respective memoirs. The humor of the situation is appreciated by both authors, who persisted in collaborating in the face of their recognition that their styles would never blend. Yeats objected to Moore's referring to the legendary characters in the play as "cattle merchants" and to the incongruity of such proposed lines as "I will kick you down the stairway of the stars,"[21] while Moore on his part complained of Yeats' thinking he was "putting style on" a manuscript when he made his heroes speak in dialect, in what Yeats thought was in the manner of Lady Gregory. Moore told Yeats that he need not think that he could acquire the dialect by going out for a walk with her.[22] All these details are known to the readers of Moore's trilogy and of Yeats' *Autobiography*. But some added light is thrown on the situation by the letters of A. E. to Yeats. For example, in two letters, one written immediately after the other, A. E. declares: "George Moore called to see me last night and I mentioned about the contions on which he might work on *Diarmuid and Grania*. He thought them reasonable, but I think the clause empowering you also to re-write rather took away his desire to do anything at it himself."[23] And the second letter:

> I returned here last night. My wife tells me that George Moore called in the afternoon and told her to tell me that he had decided to take my advice in the Yeats affair, "old friend" etc. I have not seen him yet but write to tell you of this change which I expected to come when he had brooded over what I said to him.
>
> P. S. I told Moore that if the matter was fixed up I would see that a version of it would circulate which would hurt the feelings of neither of you and that neither you nor he must claim any triumph over the other. I will, as I say, write when I see what the good man has decided. I am glad that the matter seems to be clearing up.[24]

The play was finally produced, but won no plaudits from the critics or the populace. It was said that the authors had gone to Irish legend to find in epic tradition the plot of an average French novel.[25]

Yeats felt that the effort to collaborate with Moore, which had lasted for two years, had had a permanently deleterious effect on his own style. But it was even worse, he thought, for Moore: " . . . Whatever effect that collaboration had on me it was unmixed misfortune for Moore, it set him upon a pursuit of style that made barren his later years."[26]

The attempt at collaboration ended in disappointment.[27] Had Yeats been less than the man he was, he too might have been submerged by Moore as was Martyn, who, rather than keep up the struggle with Moore, had simply given him his play, *A Tale of a Town,* to rewrite. Moore made from it *The Bending of the Bough.* The story of that struggle and its conclusion has become a legend, chiefly through the accounts of Moore and Yeats, set down in *Hail and Farewell* and *Dramatis Personae,* respectively. Moore's witty remark published in the October *Samhain* in 1901 succinctly summarizes the result. There Moore remarked that the two plays had very little in common except the names of the personages and the number of the acts.[28]

Moore's idea of collaboration is explained by Joseph Hone in his biography of George Moore. Hone says that Moore gives himself away in his short story, "Hugh Monfert," wherein Percy Knight is asked to tell "how he and his sister had achieved the difficult task of writing together. She showed me what she had written, Percy answered, and I altered it. Didn't you quarrel over the alterations? We did sometimes but in the end Beatrice saw that she was wrong."[29]

Moore's *Bending of the Bough* was chiefly his own rewriting of Martyn's *A Tale of a Town*, but Yeats asserts in his autobiography that "certain bitter sentences put into the mouth of Deane, a dramatization of Standish O'Grady," were his.[30] Yeats also says that the masterly construction of Martyn's *The Heather Field* was George Moore's.[31] If this is true, then Denis Gwynn's interpretation of the codicil of Martyn's will which bequeathed his rights in the two plays, *The Heather Field* and *Maeve*, to George Moore may be somewhat strained. Gwynn believes that Martyn meant the codicil to assert that the plays were really his own property and not the fruit of a collaboration in which Moore was the principal author, as was frequently said. If Martyn was indebted to Moore for the construction of *The Heather Field*, the codicil could have been merely an acknowledgment of Moore's rights to profits in the play.[32]

Moore is known to have asked assistance from James Stephens upon one occasion. According to Moore's biographer, Joseph Hone, he sent three of the stories of *A Story Teller's Holiday* to Stephens with a note running: "I think that if you will correct my mistakes and sprinkle the idiom over the story working it in here and there, wherever you get a chance . . . you will have accomplished the end I have in view."[33] Moore acknowledges the help given him by A. E., at the same time suggesting that James Stephens was probably the recipient of A. E.'s assistance in his early prose compositions: "What a door was opened to him when he met A. E.! Of what help A. E. was

131

to him in his first prose composition (no one can help another with poetry) none knows but Stephens himself; A. E. forgets what he gives, but it is difficult for me to believe that Stephens did not benefit enormously, as much as I did myself. How much that was I cannot tell, for A. E. was always helping me directly and indirectly."[34]

A few startling accusations of plagiarisms within the school have been made. A. E. says in a letter to Yeats that there is about a page of an essay of his in Moore's *Evelyn Innes* and that there are copious selections from a French art critic in Moore's *Modern Painting* with the quotation marks left out. "His story of *The Flood*," wrote A. E., "was also written by Zola with exactly the same plot, and I dare say any enquiring mind could multiply instances enough to make a volume showing Moore's art of selection."[35]

Yeats once approached Moore on the matter of this very accusation, that is, the plagiarism in *Modern Painting*, and, according to Yeats, Moore had been very gay about the whole thing. "The man I object to," Yeats quotes Moore as saying, "is the man who plagiarizes without knowing it; I always know; I took ten pages."[36] His admission was as frank when he said to Lady Gregory, "We both quote well, but you always put in inverted commas, I never do."[37]

But Moore adopted another tone when Lady Gregory's practice of following the translations of others was the subject of consideration. He accused Lady Gregory of slavishly following Kuno Meyer's translation of the "Wooing of Emer" in her reworking of the legend, and said that he thought she might occasionally have written "which I quote" since her practice was a "clear case of literary transubstantiation." He also condemned Yeats for upholding her in the method of piecing together portions of various French and German texts of translations from the Gaelic.[38]

Six years after Lady Gregory's death Lord Dunsany published an accusation by innuendo to the discredit of Lady Gregory. It would not do, of course, for a Lord to call directly in question the integrity of a Lady. Dunsany handles the problem with finesse, but with a suggestion of relish in the doing.

He says in his memoirs that when he presented his play, *King Argimenes,* to the Abbey, Lady Gregory indicated that it would be put on immediately, but that, for some reason that he had never understood, it had actually been delayed for a year. During that interval Lady Gregory produced a play, which she "never saw fit to print"[39] among her works, *The Deliverer.* Strangely enough, her play employed the same sort of people and the same theme that Dunsany had used in *King Argimenes.* However, there was a difference, Dunsany admits, for Lady Gregory's play ended with the king's cats, whereas his play ended with the king's dog. Dunsany's play was by this time pledged to the Abbey and he did not try to prevent its production. The week following the staging of *The Deliverer* Dunsany's cast appeared in the very same clothing that Lady Gregory's cast had worn the week before. No one contested the practicality of the costuming, since both plays dealt with the freeing of an enslaved Eastern people of the same era.[40]

Dunsany's story lends point to the dictum of A. E. Malone that *The Deliverer* was not typical of Lady Gregory's dramas because this satire on the popular treatment of the transparently disguised Parnell had a bitterness of tone quite unlike her usual manner.[41]

This was not the only time that Dunsany had provided a plot for an ambitious dramatist, as he believed. He says earlier in his memoirs that he used sometimes to talk of his plots as they occurred to him, asking advice of his elders and being discouraged. Before he had learned not to divulge his ideas to anyone "there were one or two very great successes in London made from those very plots."[42] On the other hand, he was sometimes the recipient of suggestions for drama. He says that the origin of his play about Alexander the Great was a suggestion made to him by Padraic Colum, who wished to collaborate with Dunsany on the subject. Dunsany, receptive to the idea, "read up something about him in Plutarch and began to write." He got ahead so rapidly that he asked release from his promise to collaborate, and of course Colum generously agreed.[43] Thus literary history is one instance the poorer in attempts at collaboration.

Apart from comments on collaborations and "literary tran-substantiation" many observations were made, as well as admissions granted, of reciprocal influences within the group of modern Irish writers.[44] Sometimes the influence was imposed quite consciously, as in the case of Yeats, who, according to Eglinton, "would make of the whole profession of literature one vast secret order, training its novices in the occult sciences and instructing them in a system of symbolic images, somewhat as they seem to have done in the bardic colleges of ancient Ireland."[45] Stephen Gwynn said that Yeats imposed his theories with a will of steel.[46]

Katharine Tynan was one of the first to acknowledge the influence of Yeats, dedicating a book of poetry "to W. B. Yeats who taught me." She says in her memoirs that Yeats was "the onlie begetter" of the new Irish poetry. She expressed gratitude for his delivering the poets of his generation from the insincere rhetorical passion which was suggestive of country newspaper verse.[47] In an undated letter from Yeats to Katharine Tynan, included among many from Yeats quoted in her book, *The Middle Years*,[48] he advised her to be as Irish as she was able, for by that means she would be both more original and more true to herself and "in the long run more interesting even to English readers."[49] In 1907 Yeats wrote to Katharine Tynan, openly declaring his intention of directing the labors of the younger poets: "I have plans for improving our new poets myself. I want to get them to write songs between the acts."[50] He had in mind the poets Joseph Campbell, Padraic Colum, and Lionel Johnson. So penetrating was the influence of Yeats on the Irish lyric that A. E. regretted that the poet had not preceded Moore, Mangan, and Ferguson. He felt that if they had had "so scrupulous a craftsman" for a model they would have written much greater poetry.[51]

But Yeats regretted one aspect of his influence on A. E. He deplored the fact that he had introduced A. E. to Sir Horace Plunkett, who had made him "a successful organizer of co-operative banks," thereby entangling in materialism "a mind ripe for spiritual theory."[52] A. E., however, was never dominated by

Yeats. For example, he vigorously opposed Yeats' plan for the American tour of the Abbey Theatre company. He wrote Yeats:

"I know you think, or will urge, that its work here could be helped by American success. This I do not believe . . . . Your own knowledge of the little effect your great reputation elsewhere has here ought to have taught you this."[53] Yeats' influence was largely exerted in the drama, but even in the theatre it was as a poet that his influence was felt. Padraic Colum spoke of him as that "leaven" which enabled the drama to rise above the trivially entertaining.[54]

Synge is popularly referred to as the "discovery" of Yeats, but Yeats himself uses another term. He says in *Plays and Controversies*, "Synge is a creation of our movement."[55] George Moore accuses Yeats of subjugating Synge's mind and of driving him off to Aran to primitive living conditions in the most bitter season in spite of Synge's protest that he should await the return of summer. But the usual view is that Synge's fortune was in the ascendant when chance brought him and Yeats together in Paris.[56] W. G. Fay, an eminent director of the Abbey, testifies that it was from Yeats that Synge learned such technical details as how to arrange exits and entrances, and to quicken the pace of the play by eliminating long speeches.[57]

Yet Synge at least once opposed Yeats, when Yeats had suggested adding a second company to the Abbey to play international drama. Yeats writes of the incident: "Synge, who had hitherto not opposed me . . . did so in a formal letter . . . . He said that the municipal theaters all over Europe gave fine performances of old classics, but did not create . . . and that we would create nothing if we did not give all our thoughts to Ireland."[58]

The origin of specific plays by other writers may be traced to Yeats. *John Bull's Other Island* was written by George Bernard Shaw in 1904 at the request of Yeats as a patriotic contribution to the repertory of the Irish Literary Theatre. It was Yeats who set Dunsany to writing plays. Dunsany in his memoirs attributes his first play, *The Glittering Gate,* to Yeats' insistence that he turn the theme of a picture he had drawn into drama. Dunsany had protested:

I still said that I was sure I could not write a play. There may be a certain laziness in such assumptions, as they settle definitely the question of whether or not one should work in a certain direction. Then Mr. Yeats said: "I think I must get somebody else to do it." That stung me to rise from that lethargy, for I did not want somebody else to go off with my idea. This was in the early afternoon, and during that afternoon I wrote *The Glittering Gate*. When I showed it to Mr. Yeats he told me that some dialogue would be needed while the burglar was breaking open the gate so I added a bit; but all the rest of the play was done at a sitting.[59]

Stephen Gwynn wrote plays, but when Yeats repeatedly refused to accept them for the Abbey, he finally gave up forever the idea of seeing any of his plays staged, even without remuneration, as many of those who wrote for the Abbey did see their plays produced.[60]

Yeats' influence took other than literary trends. Maud Gonne doubted whether there would have been an Easter Week had it not been for Yeats' "glorification of heroic virtue."[61] Stephen Gwynn thought that Yeats and Hyde "did not begin to count in the life of Ireland until the revolutionary movement had spent its first impetus."[62] After the land war and the Parnell agitation, the new Nationalism attracted Yeats, with the result that persons who had not been interested in him as a literary force became his professed admirers.

The contemporary critics were, however, chiefly concerned with Yeats as a force in the literary revival, and his influence over the drama was recognized by them as bound up with that of Lady Gregory, who rightly asserted that it was the existence of the Theatre which had created play-writing in Ireland. Lennox Robinson told her that his seeing the Dublin players on tour in Cork had given him the impulse to write for the theatre. His first offering, *The Clancy Name*, was altered at the suggestion of Yeats and Lady Gregory, and produced thereafter at the Abbey.[63] Padraic Colum began writing plays by the same inspiration. Lady Gregory said in her story of the theatre: "If a play shows real promise and a mind behind it, we write personally to the author, making criticisms and suggestions. We were accused for a while of smothering the work of young writers in order that we might produce our own, but time has done away with that libel."[64]

The criticisms of Yeats and Lady Gregory were at times exacting. One can only speculate as to how Synge's plays stood before they pruned away the language which they thought improper for the public ear. Lady Gregory commented on this revision:

> I remember his [Synge's] bringing the play [*The Playboy*] to us in Dublin, but he was too hoarse to read it, and it was read by Mr. Fay. We were almost bewildered by its abundance and fantasy, but we felt, and Mr. Yeats said very plainly, that there was far too much "bad language". There were too many violent oaths, and the play itself was marred by this. I did not think it was fit to be put on the stage without cutting. It was agreed that it should be cut in rehearsal . . . . I did not, however, see a rehearsal and did not hear the play again until the night of its production, and then I told Synge that the cuts were not enough, that many more should be made. He gave me leave to do this, and, in consultation with the players, I took out many phrases which, though in the printed book, have never since that first production been spoken on our stage. I am sorry they were not taken out before it had been played at all, but that is just what happened.[65]

Synge wrote to Max Meyerfeld rather humorously of his "immoral" little comedy, *The Tinker's Wedding,* placing something of compliment or slur on London, depending on the point of view: "I hope also to bring out a little two-act comedy—"The Tinker's Wedding"—very shortly . . . . We have never played it here as they say it is too immoral for Dublin! There is however some talk of having it done in London before long though nothing is decided as yet."[66]

Few, if any, will contest the fact that the "discovery" or the "creation" of Yeats and Lady Gregory was soon out of leading strings and became himself the inspiration for the whole contemporary theatre.[67] His mood turned toward realism, if not sordidness, and changed the trend of drama in Ireland. Yeats, who championed Synge even to the point of jeopardizing his own eminence as the first bard of Ireland,[68] lived to see his attempt to establish poetic drama on a secure footing fail chiefly because of the superior attraction of Synge's artistry. Moreover, Synge's influence was not confined to the drama. He influenced the whole texture of Yeats' poetry. "With Synge, dialect suddenly appears in Yeats' poetry," writes Frank O'Connor in his essay contributed to the collection, *The Irish Theatre*.[69] Although Synge's poetry had no great intrinsic merit, it influenced almost all his successors in Ireland. L. A. G. Strong says that Yeats' *Responsibilities* "shows strongly the impress of his friend's mind."[70]

A. E. was the strongest literary influence apart from the combined power of the three leaders of the dramatic movement, Yeats, Lady Gregory, and Sygne. It had been A. E.'s intention to write anonymously and he once told Yeats that if Katharine Tynan had not made his pseudonym public he would never have done so and that he would have had a much pleasanter life.[71] It is, however, highly improbable that so garrulous a man could have kept the secret, because the subject of his conversations paralleled in great measure the subject matter of his poetry.

Yeats, in recommending A. E. to Horace Plunkett, said that A. E.'s influence was involuntary.[72] A. E.'s son, Diarmuid Russell, declared him to be absolutely free of any temptation to inculcate in other poets his own ideas.[73] His influence was rather exercised by personal aid and encouragement than by imposition of literary theory or method. Stephen Gwynn feels that it was due "more to A. E.'s counsel and encouragement than to the example set by Yeats"[74] that there developed so rapidly among the Irish a skilled technique in verse. Gwynn elaborates his point, reiterating that the "effect of George Russell was an effect of saintliness."[75] It was A. E.'s philosophy, rather than his power to express this philosophy, that exerted such a profound influence on his contemporaries. He greatly influenced young Irishmen whom Yeats and Moore had not been able to impress. There is scarcely a contemporary of the mystic who has not left a testimony:

Frank O'Connor: "To that office of his people were always blowing in, uninvited and unannounced, and he always found time to talk to them. He had a multitude of acquaintances, and was the friend of every young writer who needed a friend. Almost until his death, four years ago, he read our manuscripts, found us publishers, printed our first work, supervised our reading, even tried to arrange our marriages."[76]

Lord Dunsany: "But there is another part of A. E.'s mind that I must not forget, for any account of him that neglected it would be very deficient and that is his generosity. To young poets he would give encouragement straight from the spirit, which he himself valued so much more than gold."[77] N. J. O'Connor: "The birds of 'The Shadowy Waters' surely owe much to Mr. Yeats' youthful friendship with that great Irish mystic, A. E."[78] Francis Ledwige, in the last stanza of "The Old Gods":

> Ah, foolish that I was to heed
> The voice of folly, presume
> To find the old gods in my need
> So far from A. E.'s little room.[79]

Could Yeats have been jealous of A. E.? His is the only disparaging note. Perhaps one should recall that Yeats confessed that he had always loved and hated A. E. Yeats belittles the nature of A. E.'s influence as an emanation of a religious concept rather than as a literary principle:

I once hoped a great deal from George Russell's influence. . . but he has the religious genius, and it is the essence of the religious genius, I mean the genius of the religious teacher, to look upon all souls as equal. They are never equal in the eyes of any craft, but Russell cannot bear anything that sets one man above another. He encourages everyone to write poetry because he thinks it is good for their souls, and he doesn't care a rush whether it is good or bad. When we started on the theatre he actually avowed this about plays, and tried to persuade Lady Gregory and myself to keep it a small amateur theatre that various interesting souls might be given the opportunity of dramatic expression for his soul's health . . . . The trouble is that Russell himself is absolutely charming and all the more charming because he suffers fools gladly.[80]

Poles apart from one who suffers fools gladly was George Moore, and his influence was correspondingly slight. He himself said that his novel *Esther Waters* had perhaps done more good than any other novel of his generation,[81] but Padraic Colum found Moore's novels negligible as a literary influence. "I find in these novels," wrote Colum, "a curiously alien mind. They were written in a tradition that was passing . . . ."[82] However, Arnold Bennett told St. John Ervine that he had never thought of writing about the Five Towns until Moore's *A Mummer's Wife* had revealed to him the literary significance of Staffordshire.[83]

As one looks over the whole school to evaluate the membership in terms of reputed influence, one is struck by the fact that scarcely any reference has been made to Douglas Hyde. In 1920, Padraic Colum, however, wrote of Hyde's influence on the language and metrical form of the young Irish poets. He attributed also to Hyde the young Irish poets' discovery of the racial spirit of their people.[84] Again, in 1939, he wrote more explicitly: "Douglas Hyde gave the Gaelic originals and his verse translations in his volumes of Connacht songs. He put under them a prose translation, literal but colored by Gaelic idiom. These prose translations of his suggested a new literary medium; out of them developed the poetic dialogue of Synge's plays and the narrative of Lady Gregory's stories."[85] This evaluation is a departure from the Dublin poet-critics' usual silence regarding Hyde's influence. Likewise the critics have little to say of Colum as an influence. Yet A. E. Malone attributes to him the initiating of the realistic movement in the Irish theatre.[86]

Although James Joyce is acknowledged outside of Ireland as one of the most profoundly influential writers of his century, the Irish critics of the Dublin coterie hesitated to speak of that influence. They have said not a little regarding their personal reactions to Joyce as a man and to Joyce as an artist, but few have hazarded any statements about his influence on other writers. L. A. G. Strong has said that when he was first given one of the published fragments of *Work in Progress* in his weekly batch of novels for review, he had "frankly declined to adventure." But now, he continued, he was willing to express his belief that Joyce's influence would derive from *Ulysses* and that this later technique would find few imitators. His influence,

Strong thought, would tend toward a greater flexibility of the language.[87]

Stephen Gwynn says that *Ulysses* has "affected or infected the whole of Europe" and that "all the new writers feel obliged to attempt, as it does, the doing of two things at once: moving at the same time on two (or three) distinct planes." He acknowledges that *Ulysses* has affected all theories of style.[88] John Eglinton was frankly disconcerted by the appearance of *Ulysses* with its "particularly strong and composite odour from mean streets and brothels" and expressed his doubt as to whether the work was "of good augury for Irish literature." He called the book a "violent interruption of the movement known as the Irish Literary Renascence."[89]

In March, 1934, Ernest Boyd expressed himself as unable to see that the younger Irish contemporaries had been in the least influenced by Joyce. His influence, he said, would have to be sought in England and America. He concluded positively: "In Ireland his influence has been nil."[90] But Boyd has more recently declared Sean O'Casey's *Pictures in the Hallway* to be full of "much re-Joycing, excellent, good, bad, and indifferent," particularly in such punning as O'Casey's "song-freud" and "Mariar Curehelli."[91]

In comparison with the number of critical evaluations of Joyce's influence that have appeared from the pens of English and American critics, the attention paid to Joyce in this respect by the Irish critics is slight. Perhaps the Irish were too near the author's subject matter, and were unable to get perspective because of the magnitude of his genius.

In conclusion, one may fairly assert that the Irish writers have been open and frank in their acknowledgments of suggestions received from one another, detailed in their analyses of more extended collaborations, occasionally petty in making accusations of too close imitation, and, as a rule, generous in acknowledging the extent of the influence of each poet, dramatist, or novelist. In brief, Yeats, according to his contemporaries, exerted the influence of a literary craftsman; A. E., that of spiritual guide. Synge, they said, gave a new direction to the substance of Irish drama. Lady Gregory, it appears, was influential chiefly by maintaining a theatre where young playwrights could see their dramas staged, and by keeping open house at Coole for the members of the literary school. The influence of Moore on the novel drew scant acknowledgment from his contemporaries. The poet-critics made few direct statements on the subject of Hyde's literary influence. They viewed Joyce with alarm.

NOTES

Introduction

1. Daniel Corkery, *Synge and Anglo-Irish Literature* (Cork: Cork University Press, 1931), pp. 5-6.
2. Darrell Figgis, *A. E. (George W. Russell). A Study of a Man and a Nation* (Dublin: Maunsel and Co. Ltd., 1916), p. 28.
3. Corkery, p. 3.

Chapter I

1. An interesting expression of the antithetical view is that of Havelock Ellis, who said in an article, "The Celtic Spirit in Literature," *Living Age*, CCXLVIII (March 10, 1906), 590: "I have said nothing of the 'Celtic Movement'. The reason may perhaps be clear. From the point of view of great literature there is no Celtic Movement in the petty sense in which it is generally understood, nor are great poets the outcome of such movements. If at the present time we possess one poet at all events who adequately represents the Celtic spirit, it is equally true that the same poetic qualities may be traced throughout the whole of our literature."

Lady Gregory said facetiously in *Our Irish Theatre* (New York and London: G. P. Putnam's Sons, 1913), pp. 9-10: "I think the word Celtic was put in for the sake of Fiona Macleod, whose plays, however, we never acted . . . . I myself never quite understood the meaning of the 'Celtic Movement,' which we were said to belong to. When I was asked about it, I used to say it was a movement meant to persuade the Scotch to begin buying our books, while we continued not to buy theirs."

2. George Moore, *Hail and Farewell* (New York and London: The Macmillan Co., 1924), I, 152-153. (Copyright, 1911.)
3. Padraic Colum, "Dublin in Literature," *Bookman*, LXIII (July, 1926), 556.
4. I shall hereafter refer to George William Russell as A. E.
5. William Kirkpatrick Magee is another example of one who is better known by his pen name than by his patronymic. He will be referred to hereafter as John Eglinton.
6. Although Sean O'Casey provided plays for the Abbey Theatre in the second phase of its development, he did not engage in that criticism which is the subject of this study. Neither did other celebrated Irish writers such as Sean O'Faolain and Liam O'Flaherty, for example. The list of modern Irish writers is capable of large extension, but it should be understood that only those who engaged in interchange of critical opinion and those who wrote much in comment upon those who were exchanging this criticism have a place here.

A striking juxtaposition of the more significant of these names occurs on a single page of James Joyce's *Ulysses* (New York: Random House, Modern Library edition, 1934), p. 190:

> "They say we are to have a literary surprise, the quaker librarian said, friendly and earnest. Mr. Russell, rumour has it, is gathering together a sheaf of our younger poets' verses. We are looking forward anxiously . . . .
>
> "Young Colum and Starkey. George Roberts is doing the commercial part. Longworth will give it a good puff in the *Express* . . . . I like Colum's *Drover*. Yes, I think he has that queer thing,

genius . . . . Yeats admired his line: *As in wild earth Grecian vase.*
Did he? I hope you'll be able to come tonight. Malachai Mulligan
[Gogarty] is coming too. Moore asked him to bring Haines. Did
you hear Miss Mitchell's joke about Moore and Martyn? That
Moore is Martyn's wild oats? Awfully clever, isn't it. They remind
one of don Quixote and Sancho Panza. Our national epic has yet
to be written. Dr. Sigerson says Moore is the man for it. A knight
of the rueful countenance here in Dublin . . . . James Stephens is
doing some clever sketches. We are becoming important, it
seems . . . .

"Synge has promised me an article for *Dana* too. Are we going
to be read? I feel we are. The Gaelic league wants something in
Irish. I hope you will come round tonight. Bring Starkey.

"Stephen [James Joyce] sat down.

"The quaker librarian came from the leavetakers. Blushing his
mask said:

"—Mr. Dedalus [Joyce], your views are most illuminating."

7. A. E. said of Katharine Tynan in his "Foreword" to her collected
poems: "Katharine Tynan was the earliest singer in that awakening of
our imagination which has been spoken of as the Irish Renaissance. I
think she had as much natural sunlight in her as the movement ever
attained." Katharine Tynan, *Collected Poems* (London: Macmillan and
Co., Ltd., 1930), p. vii.

8. Stephen Gwynn, *Irish Literature and Drama* (London and New
York: Thomas Nelson and Sons, Ltd., 1936), p. 126.

9. *Ibid.*, pp. 174-175.

10. Padraic Colum, *The Road Round Ireland* (New York: The Macmillan Co., 1926), p. 315.

11. Charles Duff, *James Joyce and the Plain Reader* (London: D.
Harmsworth, 1932), p. 28.

12. Figgis, *A. E.*, pp. 27-28.

13. *Ibid.*, pp. 5-6.

14. Denis Gwynn, *Edward Martyn and the Irish Revival* (London:
Jonathan Cape, 1930), p. 13.

15. *Ibid.*, p. 115.

16. That there were temperamental differences will be demonstrated
in a later chapter dealing with affinities and antipathies felt by members
of the school.

17. Denis Gwynn, *Edward Martyn*, pp. 155-156.

18. *Ibid.*, p. 157.

19. Moore, *Hail and Farewell*, I, 96.

20. William Butler Yeats, *Dramatis Personae* (New York: The Macmillan Co., 1936), p. 37.

21. Padraic Colum, "The Irish Literary Movement," *Forum*, LIII
(Jan., 1915), 148.

22. Lord Dunsany, *Patches of Sunlight* (New York: Reynal and Hitchcock, 1938), p. 136.

23. See Figgis, *A. E.*, p. 28.

24. Padraic Colum, Preface to the *Journal and Letters of Stephen
MacKenna,* edited by E. R. Dodds (New York: W. Morrow and Co., 1937),
pp. xiv-xv.

25. Moore, *Hail and Farewell*, I, 358.

26. Lord Dunsany, *My Ireland* (London and New York: Funk and
Wagnalls Co., 1937), pp. 7-8.

27. Yeats, *Dramatis Personae*, p. 72.

28. William Butler Yeats, *Autobiography* (New York: The Macmillan Co., 1938), p. 338.

Notes

29. Yeats' letter to John Quinn, quoted by Joseph Hone, in *W. B. Yeats* (New York: The Macmillan Co., 1943), p. 218.

30. See Corkery, *Synge and Anglo-Irish Literature.*

31. A. E., *Some Irish Essays* (Dublin: Maunsel and Co., Ltd., 1906), pp. 17-18.

32. William Butler Yeats, *Plays and Controversies* (London: Macmillan and Co., Ltd., 1923), p. 111.

33. Stephen Gwynn, *Experiences of a Literary Man* (New York: Henry Holt and Co., 1927), p. 71.

34. Lady Gregory, *Our Irish Theatre*, pp. 8-9.

35. Yeats, *Plays and Controversies*, p. 15.

36. *Ibid.*, p. 143.

37. *Ibid.*, pp. 9-12.

38. *Ibid.*, pp. 4-5.

39. Stephen Gwynn, *Irish Literature and Drama*, p. 151.

40. Stephen Gwynn, "The Irish Literary Theatre and Its Affinities," *Fortnightly*, LXXVI (Dec., 1901), 1052.

41. Stephen Gwynn, *Irish Literature and Drama*, p. 156.

42. Yeats, *Plays and Controversies*, p. 3.

43. Hone, *W. B. Yeats*, p. 147.

44. Colum, "The Irish Literary Movement" (see note 21, above), p. 145.

45. A. E. Malone, "The Plays of Lady Gregory," *Yale Review*, XIV, n.s. (April, 1925), 551.

46. Colum, *The Road Round Ireland*, p. 289.

47. Hone, *W. B. Yeats*, p. 454.

48. Frank O'Connor, "Two Friends: Yeats and A. E.," *Yale Review*, XXIX, n.s. (Sept., 1939), 77.

49. Hone, *W. B. Yeats*, p. 457.

50. John V. Kelleher, "Irish Literature Today," *Atlantic Monthly*, CLXXV (March, 1945), 74.

51. St. John Ervine, *The Organized Theatre* (New York: The Macmillan Co., 1924), p. 118.

52. A. E., review of Padraic Colum's *Castle Conquer*, *The Irish Statesman*, I (Oct. 6, 1923), 116. If A. E. had chosen to do so, he might also have noted the emergence of Sean O'Casey. There was little critical recognition made by members of this earlier coterie of the progenitors of the newer drama.

53. Colum, *The Road Round Ireland*, p. 284.

54. James Stephens, "The Outlook for Literature with Special Reference to Ireland," *Century*, CIV (Oct., 1922), 813.

John Eglinton wrote in the "Irish Letter," *Dial*, LXXXVI (May, 1929), 419: "We seem far enough away now from the unsubstantial hopes of the Irish Renascence."

Chapter II

1. George Bernard Shaw, *John Bull's Other Island* (London: Constable and Co., 1928), p. 16.

2. James Joyce, *A Portrait of the Artist as a Young Man* (New York: The Viking Press, *The Portable James Joyce*, 1949), p. 326. (Copyright, 1946, 1947.)
More often quoted is Stephen's announcement: "I will not serve that in which I no longer believe whether it call itself my home, my fatherland, or my church: and I will try to express myself in some mode of life or art as freely as I can and as wholly as I can, using for my defense the only arms I allow myself to use, silence, exile and cunning." *Ibid.*, p. 518.

The Modern Irish Writers

Joyce was never sentimental about Ireland. Stephen Dedalus says to Bloom, in *Ulysses:* "You suspect that I may be important because I belong to the *faubourg Saint Patrice* called Ireland for short . . . . But I suspect that Ireland must be important because it belongs to me." *Ulysses,* p. 629.

3. John Eglinton, *Irish Literary Portraits* (London: Macmillan and Co., Ltd., 1935), p. 140.

4. Frank O'Connor, "Synge" in *The Irish Theatre,* edited by Lennox Robinson (London: Macmillan and Co., Ltd., 1939).

The truth is probably more nearly approached in Joyce's record of a conversation between Dedalus and his friend Davin:

"Try to be one of us—repeated Davin—In your heart you are an Irishman but your pride is too powerful.

"My ancestors threw off their language and took another—Stephen said.—They allowed a handful of foreigners to subject them. Do you fancy I am going to pay in my own life and person debts they made? What for?

"For our freedom—said Davin.

"No honorable sincere man—said Stephen—has given up to you his life and his youth and his affections from the days of Tone to those of Parnell but you sold him to the enemy or failed him in need or reviled him and left him for another. And you invite me to be one of you. I'd see you damned first.— . . . .

"—The soul is born—he said vaguely—

"—It has a slow and dark birth, more mysterious than the birth of the body. When the soul of a man is born in this country there are nets flung at it to hold it back from flight. You talk to me of nationality, language, religion. I shall try to fly by those nets.—

". . . . Ireland first, Stevie. You can be a poet or a mystic after.—

"—Do you know what Ireland is?—asked Sephen with cold violence. Ireland is the sow that eats her farrow." *A Portrait of the Artist as a Young Man,* in *The Portable James Joyce,* pp. 467-468.

5. Moore, *Hail and Farewell,* I, 3.

6. *Ibid.,* p. 43.

7. *Ibid.,* III, 219.

8. *Ibid.,* p. 382.

9. *Ibid.,* p. 305.

10. *Ibid.,* II, 38.

11. *Ibid.,* I, 299.

12. *Ibid.,* III, 308.

13. Yeats, *Dramatis Personae,* p. 53.

14. *Journal and Letters of Stephen MacKenna,* p. 211.

15. A. E., Foreword to H. A. Law, *Anglo-Irish Literature* (New York: Longmans, Green and Co., Ltd., 1926), pp. xvi-xvii.

16. O'Connor, "Two Friends: Yeats and A. E.," *Yale Review,* XXIX, n.s. (Sept., 1939), 74.

17. A. E., Letter to Stephen Gwynn, quoted in Stephen Gwynn's *Experiences of a Literary Man,* pp. 202-203.

A. E. died in London. In his last letter, written on June 2, 1935, from his hospital bed, to Lucy Porter, he said, "But once let me get out of this city into the Irish air and I feel I could recover something at least of my old mental quickness." *A. E.'s Letters to Mináulabáin,* edited by Mrs. Kingsley Porter (New York: The Macmillan Co., 1937), p. 102.

Neither did America appeal to him. He wrote to Yeats in 1903, "I think America is an active Hell. I like the people but detest their civilization as far as I can learn anything about it. It is too noisy. I want a sleepy land like Ireland to live in." *Some Passages from the Letters of A.E. to W. B. Yeats* (Dublin: The Cuala Press, 1936), p. 41.

18. Hone, *W. B. Yeats*, p. 361.

19. L. A. G. Strong, "W. B. Yeats," in *Scattering Branches: Tributes to the Memory of W. B. Yeats*, ed. by Stephen Gwynn (New York: The Macmillan Co.), p. 188.

20. Letter from Yeats to Katharine Tynan, quoted in Katharine Tynan (Hinkson), *The Middle Years* (London: Constable and Co. Ltd., 1916), p. 63.

21. Stephen Gwynn, *Today and Tomorrow in Ireland* (Dublin: Hodges, Figgis and Co., Ltd., 1903), pp. ix-x.

22. Darrell Figgis, *Studies and Appreciations* (London: J. M. Dent and Sons, Ltd., 1912), p. 24.

23. John Eglinton, *Bards and Saints* (Dublin: Maunsel and Co., Ltd., 1906), p. 36.

24. Eglinton, *Irish Literary Portraits*, p. 10.

Chapter III

1. A. E., "Anglo-Irish Literature," *Irish Statesman*, VII (Jan. 22, 1927), 477-478.

2. Yeats, *Autobiography*, p. 403.

3. See "September, 1913" in *The Collected Poems of W. B. Yeats* (New York: The Macmillan Co., 1940), p. 122.

4. William Butler Yeats, *The Celtic Twilight* (London: A. H. Bullen, 1902), pp. 135-136.

5. William Butler Yeats, Preface, *The Unicorn from the Stars* (New York: The Macmillan Co., 1908), p. vi: ". . . for the public mind of Ireland, stupefied by prolonged intolerant organization, can take but brief pleasure in the caprice that is in all art, whatever its subject, and, more commonly can but hate unaccustomed personal reverie."

6. Yeats, *Autobiography*, pp. 402-403.

7. W. B. Yeats, "J. M. Synge and the Ireland of his Time," *Forum*, XLVI (Aug., 1911), 197.

8. Yeats, *Autobiography*, pp. 443-444. This theory of the generative power of oppositional temperament is much the same as that expressed by A. E. in his advice to Frank O'Connor.

9. Hone, *W. B. Yeats*, p. 371.

10. Joyce, *A Portrait of the Artist as a Young Man*, in *The Portable James Joyce*, p. 467.

11. Yeats, *Dramatis Personae*, p. 80.

12. Maud Gonne, "Yeats and Ireland," in *Scattering Branches*, p. 20.

13. The earliest of the Irish Literary Theatre pamphlets, which was followed in turn by *Samhain* and *The Arrow*, irregular publications of the movement.

14. A. E. Malone. *The Irish Drama* (London: Constable and Co., Ltd., 1929), p. 81.

15. A. E., letter to Kingsley Porter, Sept. 21, 1932, in *A. E.'s Letters to Minánlabáin*, p. 56.

16. Yeats, *Collected Poems*, p. 93.

17. Yeats was a member of the Senate of the *Dail Eireann* of the Irish Free State.

18. *Samhain* (Nov., 1908), p. 7.

19. A. E., *The Living Torch* (New York: The Macmillan Co., 1938), p. 183.

20. A. E., *Some Irish Essays*, p. 13.

21. *Ibid.*, p. 15.

22. See A. E., "Anglo-Irish Literature" (see note 1, above), p. 478.

23. R. C. Feld, "The Opinions of A. E.," *Century Magazine,* CIII (Nov., 1921), 6-7.

24. Lord Dunsany, *My Ireland,* p. 8.

25. *Ibid.,* pp. 39-40.

26. *Ibid.,* p. 40.

Lord Dunsany utilized Oriental settings in a few of his plays, notably *If* and *The Tents of the Arabs,* but this literary artifice, which is similar to that employed by James Hilton in *Lost Horizon,* is not what is meant by A. E.'s "Orientalism." Dunsany is referring to that organic mysticism of A. E. which was inseparable from his being.

John Eglinton said of Yeats: "It was from the East that Yeats snatched the clue to the interpretation of the Druidic culture; it was Theosophy which was able to supplement the scanty hint of the Druidic mysteries vouchsafed by Julius Caesar, and to furnish a living system of arcane teaching. Yeats' early poems are in fact as full of Hinduism as of Celticism." *Irish Literary Portraits,* p. 23.

27. St. John Ervine, *Some Impressions of My Elders* (New York: The Macmillan Co., 1922), p. 58.

28. Moore, *Hail and Farewell,* I, 150.

29. *Ibid.,* p. 36.

30. *Ibid.,* p. 129.

31. *Ibid.,* p. 57.

32. *Ibid.,* p. 160.

33. Susan Mitchell, *George Moore* (New York: Dodd, Mead and Co., 1916), p. 68.

34. *Ibid.,* pp. 59-60.

35. John Eglinton, "George Moore and Holy Ireland," *Dial,* LXXXVI (April, 1929), 341.

36. *Ibid.,* p. 342.

37. John Eglinton, Preface to *Anglo Irish Essays* (New York: John Lane Co., 1918), p. 4.

38. *Ibid.,* pp. 39-40.

39. Oliver St. John Gogarty, *Going Native* (New York: Duell, Sloan and Pearce, 1940), pp. 14-15.

40. Oliver St. John Gogarty, *I Follow St. Patrick* (New York: Reynal and Hitchcock, 1938), pp. 286-287.

It is in this book that Gogarty set down his conviction that St. Patrick was born in St. David's, Wales. L. S. Gógan of the Department of Education of the National Museum of Ireland, in an article in the *Irish Ecclesiastical Record* of March, 1950, lends support to Gogarty's theory. In a letter to me dated July 20, 1953, Mr. Gógan replied to my query relative to this support: "In listing the various views as to the birthplace I included Dr. Gogarty's, somewhat aciduously I fear, but with due credit for getting nearer the facts than the rest of a somewhat portentous band of scholars, chiefly, I indicate, without studying the problem at all!" The Welsh origins theory furnishes a rather amusing situation when juxtaposed to this delineation of the Irish as the expression of the spirit of St. Patrick.

41. Gogarty, *Going Native,* p. 19.

42. James Stephens, "Irish Letter," *Dial,* LXXVI (May, 1924), 524-525.

43. Strong, "W. B. Yeats," in *Scattering Branches,* p. 189.

44. *Ibid.,* p. 189.

45. Katharine Tynan (Hinkson), *Twenty-five Years* (London: Smith, Elder and Co., 1913), p. 142.

46. *Ibid.,* p. 122.

47. A. E. Malone, "The Plays of Lady Gregory," *Yale Review,* XIV, n.s. (1925), 545.

Notes

48. Malone, *The Irish Drama*, p. 262.
49. Malone, "The Rise of the Realistic Movement," in *The Irish Theatre*, p. 113.
50. Stephen Gwynn, *Irish Literature and Drama*, p. 202.
51. Stephen Gwynn, *Today and Tomorrow in Ireland*, p. 36.

Chapter IV

1. Moore, *Hail and Farewell*, I, 154.
2. Hone, *W. B. Yeats*, p. 481.
3. William Butler Yeats, *The King of the Great Clock Tower, Commentaries and Poems* (New York: The Macmillan Co., 1935), pp. 29-30.
4. *Some Passages from the Letters of A. E. to W. B. Yeats*, p. 62.
5. *A. E.'s Letters to Minánlabáin*, p. 46.
6. *Ibid.*, p. 41.
7. *Journal and Letters of Stephen MacKenna*, p. 208.
8. Moore, *Hail and Farewell*, II, 357.
9. O'Connor, "Two Friends: Yeats and A. E.," *Yale Review*, XXIX, n.s. (Sept., 1939), 80.
10. Yeats, "J. M. Synge and the Ireland of his Time," *Forum*, XLVI (Aug., 1911), 184-185.
11. Samuel Synge, *Letters to My Daughter* (Dublin and Cork: The Talbot Press, Ltd., 1932), pp. 36-37.
12. *Journal and Letters of Stephen MacKenna*, p. 39.
13. See Denis Gwynn, *Edward Martyn*, pp. 29-30.
14. Moore, *Hail and Farewell*, I, 315-316.
15. *Ibid.*
16. Lady Gregory, *Our Irish Theatre*, p. 27.
17. Malone, *The Irish Drama*, p. 161.
18. Lady Gregory, Preface, *The Kiltartan Poetry Book* (New York and London: G. P. Putnam's Sons, 1919), pp. 7-8.
19. Eglinton, *Irish Literary Portraits*, p. 34.
20. *Ibid.*, p. 52.
21. John Eglinton, "The Modern Irishman and the Mere Irishman," *Living Age*, CCXCI (Nov. 18, 1916), 428.
22. Eglinton, *Anglo-Irish Essays*, pp. 5-6.
23. Lord Dunsany, *My Ireland*, p. 276.
24. Francis Hackett, Introduction to Oliver St. John Gogarty's *As I Was Going down Sackville Street* (London: Rich and Cowan, Ltd., 1937), p. ix.
25. Stephen Gwynn, *Irish Literature and Drama*, pp. 158-159.
26. Gogarty, *Going Native*, pp. 8-10.
27. Yeats, *Plays and Controversies*, p. 41.
28. Protestants, as a class, opposed separation from England.
29. Not to be confused with the New Army Republicans whom De Valera had repudiated for their outlawry.

Chapter V

1. The Gaelic League was founded by Douglas Hyde, David Comyn, Father Eugene O'Growney, and Eoin MacNeill in 1893 for the purpose of preserving the age-long cultural identity of the Irish nation toward which the Irish themselves were growing apathetic as the English language and culture became increasingly the shaping forces in Ireland. With a small band of enthusiastic scholars and literary men as followers, Hyde set in motion the movement which, though not political in its initial intention, yielded large fruit in political consequence.

The Modern Irish Writers

2. In 1905 the Sinn Fein movement, based on the cultural policy of the Gaelic League, but aiming at political independence, began a period of activity which culminated in the establishment of the Irish Volunteers in 1913. The object of the Volunteers was to resist by force the autonomy of the English government. The insurrections of 1916 and 1921 were the work of this comparatively small body of men, the Irish Volunteers.

3. The Famine, usually referred to as a proper noun, was occasioned by the failure of the potato crop in the years 1845-1847. The consequent depopulation by death and emigration reduced the population of Ireland by 50 per cent.

4. Not to be confused with *Literary Ideals in Ireland*, a gathering which preceded *Ideals in Ireland*. The latter publication deals almost exclusively with the revival of Gaelic.

5. *Ideals in Ireland*, edited by Lady Gregory (London: At the Unicorn, VII Cecil Court, 1901), p. 55.

6. Stephen Gwynn, *Irish Literature and Drama*, p. 132.

7. Denis Gwynn, *Edward Martyn*, p. 255.

8. Colum, *The Road Round Ireland*, p. 470.

9. Stephen Gwynn, *Experiences of a Literary Man*, p. 68.

10. Hyde himself called Trinity College "that English fort . . . blinded with politics and religious bigotry" (*Ideals in Ireland*, p. 61).

11. Yeats, *Dramatis Personae*, p. 15.

12. Denis Gwynn, *Edward Martyn*, p. 239.

13. Stephen Gwynn, *Experiences of a Literary Man*, p. 259.

14. Katharine Tynan, *Twenty-five Years*, p. 123.

15. Hone, *W. B. Yeats*, p. 108.

16. Lady Gregory, *Our Irish Theatre*, p. 76.

17. George Moore, "A Plea for the Soul of the Irish People," *Nineteenth Century*, XLIX (Feb., 1901), 293.

18. Stephen Gwynn, *Today and Tomorrow in Ireland*, p. 74.

19. *Ideals in Ireland, passim*. See also Yeats, "Literature and the Living Voice," *Contemporary Review*, XC (1906), 472-482.

20. Yeats, *Dramatis Personae*, p. 49.

21. Susan Mitchell, *George Moore*, p. 64.

22. Eglinton, *Irish Literary Portraits*, pp. 87-88.

23. "Literary Notes," *Dublin Penny Journal* (April 5, 1902), p. 5.

24. Moore, *Hail and Farewell*, I, 1.

25. *Ibid.*, p. 4.

26. Stephen Gwynn, "The Irish Literary Theatre and its Affinities," *Fortnightly*, LXXVI (1901), 1054.

27. Stephen Gwynn, *Irish Literature and Drama*, p. 165.

28. Moore, *Hail and Farewell*, I, 96-97.

29. William Archer, "Real Conversations," *Critic*, XXXIX (July, 1901), p. 51.

30. Moore, "A Plea for the Soul of the Irish People" (see note 17, above), p. 287.

31. *Ibid.*, p. 289.

32. *Ibid.*, p. 287.

33. *Ibid.*, p. 294.

34. Moore, *Hail and Farewell*, I, 341.

35. *Ibid.*, I, 159.

36. Denis Gwynn, *Edward Martyn*, p. 239.

37. *Ibid.*

38. Eglinton, *Irish Literary Portraits*, pp. 86-87.

Eglinton implies that it was Yeats who instigated Moore to make an attack on Mahaffy which Moore was later to regret because of the isolation he suffered in Dublin as a result.

Notes

39. W. B. Yeats, "Literature and the Living Voice," *Contemporary Review*, XC (1906), 473.
40. *Ibid.*, pp. 473-474.
41. Hone, *Yeats*, p. 379.
42. A. E., in *Ideals in Ireland*, p. 19.
43. A. E., *The Living Torch*, p. 219.
44. *Ibid.*, p. 238.
45. *Ibid.*, p. 240.
46. Moore, *Hail and Farewell*, II, 40.
47. *Ibid.*, I, 165.
48. Feld, "The Opinions of A. E.," *Century*, CIII (1921), 7.
49. A. E., "Irish Anticipations," *Survey*, XLVII (Nov. 26, 1921), 291.
50. *Journal and Letters of Stephen MacKenna*, p. 122.
51. *Ibid.*, p. 216.
52. Colum, Preface, *Journal and Letters of Stephen MacKenna*, p. xiii.
53. See E. R. Dodds, "Memoir," in *Journal and Letters of Stephen MacKenna*, pp. 36-37.
54. Stephen MacKenna, the translator of Plotinus, should not be confused with Stephen McKenna, the novelist.
55. Colum, Preface, *Journal and Letters of Stephen MacKenna*, p. xiv.
56. Padraic Colum, "The Promise of Irish Letters," *Nation*, CXVII (Oct. 10, 1923), 397.
57. Eglinton, *Irish Literary Portraits*, p. 4.
58. John Eglinton, "Dublin Letter," *Dial*, LXXII (June, 1922), 621.
59. Moore, *Hail and Farewell*, I, 166.
60. Eglinton, *Bards and Saints*, p. 11.
61. *Ibid.*, p. 12.
62. *Ibid.*, p. 7.
63. Eglinton, *Anglo-Irish Essays*, pp. 29-33. This essay was first published in 1901 and was reprinted in 1917 and 1918.
64. James Joyce, *Stephen Hero* (New York: New Directions Press, 1944), p. 46.
65. *Ibid.*, p. 54.
66. *Ibid.*, p. 56.
67. Padraic Colum, "Ulysses in its Epoch," *Saturday Review of Literature* (Jan. 27, 1934), 438.
68. Joyce, *Ulysses*, p. 672.
69. *Ibid.*, p. 16.
70. Gogarty, *Going Native*, p. 21.
71. Ervine, *Some Impressions of My Elders*, p. 171.
72. *Ibid.*, pp. 49-50.
73. "Approximately 12,500 teachers have already qualified to teach the language. The use of Irish as a medium of instruction in the schools continues to increase." *The Statesman's Yearbook*, 1944, p. 475.
"Gaelic is gradually supplanting English as the medium of instruction." *New International Year Book*, 1945, p. 185.

Chapter VI

1. W. B. Yeats, "Introduction to Mandookya Upanishad," *Criterion*, XIV (July, 1935), 548.
2. Moore, *Hail and Farewell*, III, 202.
3. Colum, *The Road Round Ireland*, pp. 358-359.
4. Gogarty, *As I Was Going down Sackville Street*, p. 289.
5. Mary Colum, "Shaw and Synge," *Forum*, XCIV (Dec., 1935), 357.
6. Yeats, "J. M. Synge and the Ireland of His Time," *Forum*, XLVI (1911), 195-196.

7. Gogarty, *As I Was Going down Sackville Street,* p. 180.
8. The poem first appeared in *Irish Statesman,* IX (Jan. 21, 1928), 457.
9. John Quinn, in *The Irish Home Rule Convention* (New York: The Macmillan Co., 1917), pp. 82-83.
10. Stephen Gwynn, "Ebb and Flow," *Fortnightly,* CXLIV, n.s. (Dec., 1938), 743. The lines he had quoted were: "No pride hath he who sings of escape from love; All songs of escape from love are songs of despair; Who so hath got him away hath got nowhere."
11. Eglinton, *Irish Literary Portraits,* p. 85.
12. Yeats, *Autobiography,* p. 384.
13. A. E., *Some Irish Essays,* p. 11.
14. A. E., review of Oliver Gogarty's *An Offering of Swans, Irish Statesman,* I (Dec. 15, 1923), 436.
15. Padraic Colum, "A. E.," *New Republic,* XV (June 8, 1918), 174.
16. Eglinton, *Irish Literary Portraits,* p. 139. The reference to the tenor voice would be understood by Dubliners who not only knew that Joyce had a fine tenor voice, but also knew that the local celebrity, Dr. Mahaffy of Trinity College, used to say that he had never known a young man with a good tenor voice who did not go to the devil.
17. *Ibid.,* p. 140.
18. *Ibid.,* p. 141.
19. Gogarty, *As I Was Going down Sackville Street,* p. 285.
20. Colum, *The Road Round Ireland,* p. 313.
21. Moore, *Hail and Farewell,* III, 219.
22. Colum, "A. E.," *New Republic,* XV (1918), 173.
23. Ervine, *Some Impressions of My Elders,* p. 34.
24. Moore, *Hail and Farewell,* I, 156.
25. Gogarty, *As I Was Going down Sackville Street,* p. 20.
26. Eglinton, *Irish Literary Portraits,* p. 28.
27. L. A. G. Strong, "John Millington Synge," *Bookman,* LXXIII (April, 1931), 134.
28. Moore, Preface to Edward Martyn, *The Heather Field* (London: Duckworth and Co., 1899), p. xx. This effusiveness contrasts strangely with Moore's reference to the play, in 1911, in *Hail and Farewell,* I, 170: "He [Martyn] was to me a pathetic figure as he sat sunning himself in the light of Ibsen and Parnell, his exterior placid as a parish priest's; for knowing him from the very beginning of his life, and having seen the play written, I was not duped like the others."
Although not exactly comparing himself to Apuleius, Moore said that *The Golden Ass* was just such a book as he himself would have written had he lived a thousand years earlier. See "A Dedication to Robert Ross," *A Mummer's Wife* (London: William Heinemann, 1885), p. ix.
29. *Ibid.,* p. 20.
30. Colum, *The Road Round Ireland,* p. 279.
31. *Ibid.,* p. 311.
32. Ervine, *The Organized Theatre,* p. 27.
33. John Eglinton, "Yeats and His Story," *Dial,* LXXX (May, 1926), 358. Also in *Anglo-Irish Essays,* p. 87.
34. Stephen Gwynn, "The Irish Literary Theatre and Its Affinities," *Fortnightly,* LXXVI (1901), 1062.
35. Ervine, *Some Impressions of My Elders,* p. 183.
36. A. E., review of James Stephens' *In the Land of Youth, Irish Statesman,* III (Nov. 8, 1924), 278.
37. W. G. Fay, "The Poet and the Actor," in *Scattering Branches,* p. 129.
38. Strong, "W. B. Yeats," in *Scattering Branches,* p. 226.

39. Stephen Gwynn, "Scattering Branches," in *Scattering Branches,* p. 8.

40. *Ibid.,* pp. 5-6.

41. James Joyce, "The Day of the Rabblement," reproduced in part by Herbert Gorman in *James Joyce* (New York: Farrar and Rinehart, Inc., 1939), pp. 71-72.

42. A. E., review of Padraic Colum's *Castle Conquer,* p. 116.

43. Yeats, Note to *Plays in Prose and Verse* (New York: The Macmillan Co., 1928), p. 425.

44. Stephen Gwynn, *Today and Tomorrow in Ireland,* p. 45. The italics are mine.

45. Moore, *Hail and Farewell,* III, 257.

46. Katharine Tynan, *Twenty-five Years,* p. 254.

47. Stephens, "The Outlook for Literature, with Special Reference to Ireland," *Century,* CIV (1922), 811.

48. A. E., *The National Being* (New York: The Macmillan Co., 1937), pp. 23-24.

Chapter VII

1. Yeats, *Autobiography,* p. 369.

James Stephens said in his article, "Dublin," *The Living Age,* CCCIV (Jan. 17, 1920), 168-169:

"Dublin is less an aggregation of buildings than a collection of personages . . . .

"Where but in Dublin will you meet the author of a ballad in a thousand limericks, each verse of which is better than the last by the sheer merit of being worse; or the scholar who could have been a saint but that he preferred to be a wit, and is jeopardizing even that by a lust for the concertina; or the dramatist who marches thinly, the very wraith and apparition of himself, solid only by his boots? There is the distinguished nobleman who looks like the Wild Man from Borneo, and the other distinguished gentleman who looks like a pair of spats. Mr. Yeats will pass like something that has just been dreamed into existence by himself, and for which he has not yet found the precisely fantastic adjective. A. E. will jog along, confiding either a joke or poem into his own beard, the sole person in the street who is not aware that he is famous."

2. Moore, *Hail and Farewell,* III, 175.

3. "He is not satisfied with his portrait, and complains that I have represented him in *Ave* and *Salve* as the blameless hero of a young girl's novel.

" 'Why have you found no fault with me? If you wish to create human beings you must discover their faults.' " Moore, *Hail and Farewell,* III, 254.

Yeats, in a letter to Dorothy Wellesley, records a conversation between him and his wife soon after the death of A. E.: "My wife said the other night, 'A. E. was the nearest to a saint you or I will ever meet. You are a better poet but no saint. I suppose one has to choose.' " *Letters on Poetry from W. B. Yeats to Dorothy Wellesley* (London: Oxford University Press, 1940), p. 13.

The appellation of "saint" has high frequency in criticisms of A. E. by all the various members of the school. Yeats said in "More Memories," *Dial,* LXXIII (July, 1922), 51: "George Russell was, in the eyes of the community, saint and genius."

4. Joyce, *Ulysses,* p. 139.

5. *Ibid.*, p. 131.

6. George Moore, *Evelyn Innes* (New York and London: D. Appleton and Co., 1915), pp. 162-163. In later editions Ulick is amended. He becomes a blend of Yeats and A. E. Moore gives him a beard and old casual clothes, and in the conversational matter Moore drops out Ulick's [i.e., Yeats'] views on Shakespeare, Blake, and Shelley.

7. Compare with treatments of Yeats' aloofness in the latter half of this chapter.

8. Gogarty, *Going Native*, pp. 4-6.

9. *A. E.'s Letters to Minánlabáin*, p. 54.

10. Moore, *Hail and Farewell*, III, 258.

11. *Ibid.*, I, 159.

12. *Ibid.*, I, 280.

13. *Ibid.*, I, 285-286.

14. *Ibid.*, I, 169.

15. *Ibid.*, I, 167.

16. *Ibid.*, I, 164.

17. Lucy Kingsley Porter, Introduction to *A. E.'s Letters to Minánlabáin*, p. 14.

18. Feld, "The Opinions of A. E.," *Century*, CIII (1921), 4.

19. Padraic Colum, "Dr. Hyde of Eire," *Commonweal*, XXX (June 2, 1939), 146.

20. Yeats, *Autobiography*, p. 361.

21. Oliver St. John Gogarty, "Next Door to George Moore," *Saturday Review of Literature*, XIV (July 18, 1936), 3.

22. Edward Martyn, *The Dream Physician* (New York: Brentano's, 1918), p. 43.

23. Eglinton, *Irish Literary Portraits*, p. 118.

24. Joyce, *Ulysses*, p. 205.

25. *Ibid.*, p. 5.

26. *Ibid.*, p. 7.

27. *Ibid.*, p. 206.

28. *Ibid.*, p. 410. Students of Joyce will enjoy the trans-reference of Oliver to Roland, typical of his associational method.

29. *Ibid.*, p. 163.

30. *Ibid.*, p. 189. The reference is to A. E.'s practical concern with national co-operatives at the same time that he was indulging in experiments in the occult. At this period, 1906, A. E.'s talk ran on his philosophy of the Shadow and its relation to the Substance. Stephen Gwynn draws upon this current conversation for building up the central figure in his novel, *The Old Knowledge*.

31. Eglinton, *Irish Literary Portraits*, p. 17.

32. Stephen Gwynn, "Scattering Branches," in *Scattering Branches*, p. 5.

33. Stephen Gwynn, *Irish Literature and Drama*, p. 121.

34. Stephen Gwynn, *Experiences of a Literary Man*, p. 150.

35. Ervine, *Some Impressions of My Elders*, pp. 301-303.

36. *Ibid.*, p. 274.

37. *Ibid.*, p. 264.

38. *Ibid.*, pp. 298-299.

39. Moore, *Evelyn Innes*, pp. 235-236. Since the novel was published in 1898, it is evident that this is the youthful poet. The Yeats of whom Ervine was writing was the mature man, the acknowledged leader of dramatic enterprise in Dublin.

40. O'Connor, "Two Friends: Yeats and A. E.," *Yale Review*, XXIX, n.s. (1939), 77.

41. Hone, *W. B. Yeats*, p. 233.

42. Lady Gregory, *Our Irish Theatre*, pp. 28-29.

Notes

43. Gogarty, *I Follow St. Patrick,* pp. 143-144.
44. Gogarty, *Going Native,* p. 12.
45. Maud Gonne, "Yeats and Ireland," in *Scattering Branches,* p. 29.
46. F. R. Higgins, "Yeats as Irish Poet," in *Scattering Branches,* pp. 152-153.
47. A. E., "The Memories of a Poet," *Irish Statesman,* VII (Dec. 4, 1926), 302.
48. Strong, "W. B. Yeats," in *Scattering Branches,* p. 226.
49. *Ibid.,* pp. 195-196.
50. Lennox Robinson, "The Man and the Dramatist," in *Scattering Branches,* pp. 59-63.
51. Yeats, *Autobiography,* pp. 196-197.
52. *Ibid.,* pp. 417-418.
53. Hone, *W. B. Yeats,* p. 244.
54. Yeats, *Autobiography,* p. 401.
55. Katharine Tynan, *The Middle Years,* p. 44. The letter is dated Aug. 30, 1888.
56. *Letters on Poetry from W. B. Yeats to Dorothy Wellesley,* p. 41. The letter is dated Nov. 15, 1935.
57. *Ibid.,* pp. 43-44. The latter is dated Nov. 28, 1935.
58. *Ibid.,* p. 176.

Chapter VIII

1. *A. E.'s Letters to Minánlabáin,* p. 67. The letter is dated Dec. 16, 1932.
2. O'Connor, "Two Friends: Yeats and A. E.," *Yale Review,* XXIX, n.s. (1939), 76.
3. Hone, *W. B. Yeats,* p. 474.
4. *Ibid.,* p. 129.
5. Dodds, "Memoir," *Journal and Letters of Stephen MacKenna,* p. 36.
6. Moore, *Hail and Farewell,* III, 252.
7. *Ibid.,* p. 250.
8. Shaw Desmond, "Dunsany, Yeats, and Shaw," *Bookman,* LVIII (Nov., 1923), 263.
9. Moore, *Hail and Farewell,* III, 251-252.
10. April, 1902.
11. Yeats, *Autobiography,* p. 384.
12. *Ibid.,* p. 385. The italics are mine.
13. *Ibid.,* p. 384.
14. Gogarty, *As I Was Going down Sackville Street,* p. 169.
15. Moore, *Hail and Farewell,* III, 260.
16. L. A. G. Strong says that Moore caused A. E. to protect himself at law against a projected chapter of *Hail and Farewell* which alleged that he neglected his wife in favor of another lady. *Scattering Branches,* p. 220.
17. Moore, *Hail and Farewell,* II, 19.
18. *Ibid.,* II, 34.
19. *Ibid.,* p. 103.
20. O'Connor, "Two Friends: Yeats and A. E." (see note 2, above), pp. 69-70.
21. Stephen Gwynn, *Experiences of a Literary Man,* pp. 200-201.
22. Extract from a letter from A. E. to Stephen Gwynn, quoted in Gwynn's *Experiences of a Literary Man,* p. 202.
23. Katharine Tynan (Hinkson), *The Years of the Shadow* (London: Constable and Co., Ltd., 1919), p. 24.
24. See Joyce, *Ulysses,* p. 183. A resumé of Russell's conversation appears in more extended form on page 184.

25. O'Connor, "Two Friends: Yeats and A. E." (see note 2, above), pp. 64-65.

26. *Some Passages from the Letters of A. E. to W. B. Yeats*, p. 38.

27. Speaking of the scant number of literary men in attendance at the funeral of George Moore at the crematorium at Golders Green close to Hampstead Heath, S. K. Ratcliffe says, "It is astonishing, unless one should choose to lay emphasis on the fact that 'our dear brother here departed' was a writer who quarreled lustily through sixty years and found continuous delight in forging and launching the hardest insults at his fellows," that "no member of the Irish group which made the gossip of literary Dublin more entertaining and more malicious than that of any other capital during many years before the war" attended. "George Moore's Burial," *Nation*, CXXXVI (Feb. 22, 1933), 205.

Gogarty remarks in *I Follow St. Patrick* that he was one of three persons outside the family invited to attend the funeral of George Moore, whose ashes were buried on Castle Island "in an urn of brown clay, fashioned after the fashion of the ancient Gaels" (p. 215).

28. George Moore, *A Communication to My Friends* (London: The Nonesuch Press, 1933), p. 79.

29. Moore, *Hail and Farewell*, I, 287.

30. *Ibid.*, III, 182.

31. *Ibid.*, III, 208.

32. *Ibid.*, III, 186.

33. *Ibid.*, III, 220.

34. *Ibid.*, I, 49-50.

35. Ervine, *Some Impressions of My Elders*, pp. 161-162.

36. Yeats, *Plays and Controversies*, p. 156.

37. William Butler Yeats, *Wheels and Butterflies* (New York: The Macmillan Co., 1935), p. 126.

38. Yeats, "The Cat and the Moon," in *Wheels and Butterflies*, pp. 131-132.

39. Yeats, *Autobiography*, p. 346.

40. *Ibid.*, p. 378.

41. Moore, *Hail and Farewell*, III, 144.

42. Yeats, *Autobiography*, p. 369.

43. Robinson, "Scattering Branches," in *Scattering Branches*, p. 65.

44. Ervine, *Some Impressions of My Elders*, p. 162.

45. Yeats, *Autobiography*, p. 370.

46. Gerald Cumberland, "The Amazing Dubliners," *The Century*, CI (Jan., 1921), 315.

47. See Gogarty, *As I Was Going down Sackville Street*, p. 249.

48. *Ibid.*, p. 113.

49. Joseph Hone, *The Life of George Moore* (London: V. Gollancz, Ltd., 1936), p. 265.

50. Ervine, *Some Impressions of My Elders*, p. 188.

51. Eglinton, *Irish Literary Portraits*, p. 101.

52. Moore, *Hail and Farewell*, III, 260.

53. *Ibid.*, pp. 263-264. Moore was probably thinking of the primitive dugouts found preserved in peat bogs of which several are now on display in the Dublin museum. By this time Moore thought of the Gaelic language as about as practical in revival as the old dugout would be for modern commerce.

54. Yeats, *Autobiography*, p. 343. Yeats used this same phrasing in his youthful novel, *John Sherman*, of Sherman and his friend Howard: "Their friendship was founded in a great measure on mutual contempt." *The Collected Works of W. B. Yeats* (Stratford-on-Avon: The Shakespeare Head Press, 1909), VIII, 265.

Notes

55. Yeats, *Autobiography*, p. 343.
56. Moore, *Hail and Farewell*, III, 268-269.
57. Hone, *W. B. Yeats*, p. 134.
58. Quoted by Denis Gwynn in *Edward Martyn*, p. 33.
59. Moore, *Hail and Farewell*, I, 81-82.
60. Eglinton, *Irish Literary Portraits*, pp. 137-138.
61. Gogarty, *As I Was Going down Sackville Street*, p. 284.
62. Joyce, *Ulysses*, p. 213.
Mary Colum in an article entitled "Lady Gregory of the Abbey Theater," in *Tomorrow*, IV (Feb., 1945), 20-24, further attests to the prejudice against Lady Gregory. She quotes a member of the early Abbey group as saying that although Lady Gregory's diplomacy was successful, "'because it combined resolution with an artlessness of manner and a flattery of address, it was very annoying. She had kindly, friendly eyes, but a mouth that was inflexible'" (p. 21).
63. Colum, *The Road Round Ireland*, p. 316.
64. Padraic Colum, "Oliver Gogarty on James Joyce," *Saturday Review of Literature*, XXIII (Feb. 22, 1941), 11.
65. Hone, *W. B. Yeats*, pp. 311-312.
66. Eglinton, *Irish Literary Portraits*, pp. 136-137.
67. Joyce, *Ulysses*, p. 87.
68. *Ibid.*, p. 604.
69. *Ibid.*, p. 605.
70. *Ibid.*, pp. 604-605.
71. *Ibid.*, p. 649.
72. Gogarty, *As I Was Going down Sackville Street*, pp. 286-287.
73. Yeats, "J. M. Synge and the Ireland of his Time," *Forum*, XLVI (1911), 191-192.
74. Lady Gregory, *Our Irish Theatre*, pp. 122-123.
75. Strong, "John Millington Synge," *Bookman*, LXXIII (1931), 126.
76. Gogarty, *As I Was Going down Sackville Street*, p. 283.
77. Dodds, "Memoir," *Journal and Letters of Stephen MacKenna*, p. 11.
78. *Ibid.*, p. 78.
79. *Ibid.*, p. 65.

Chapter IX

1. Yeats said in 1897 in "The Celtic Element in Literature," reprinted in 1914 in *Ideas of Good and Evil:* "The reaction against the rationalism of the eighteenth century has mingled with a reaction against the materialism of the nineteenth century, and the symbolical movement, which has come to perfection in Germany in Wagner, in England in the Pre-Raphaelites, and in France in Villiers de L'Isle Adam, and Mallarmé and Maeterlinck, and has stirred the imagination of Ibsen and D'Annunzio, is certainly the only movement that is saying new things." *Ideas of Good and Evil* (London: A. H. Bullen, 1914), p. 204.
"The test of poetry is not in reason but in a delight not different from the delight that comes to a man at the first coming of love into the heart." William Butler Yeats, *The Cutting of an Agate* (New York: The Macmillan Co., 1912), p. 81.
"We cannot discover our subject matter by deliberate intellect . . . ." *Ibid.*, p. 101.
2. Hone, *W. B. Yeats*, p. 90.
3. Yeats, "The Philosophy of Shelley's Poetry," in *Ideas of Good and Evil*, p. 80.
4. *Ibid.*, p. 90. Moore reports Yeats as having said that the dropping of ideas out of literature would be a pure benefit, that modern literature

was dying of ideas, that the literature which has come down to us is free from ideas, and that ideas are the portion of vestrymen. See *Hail and Farewell*, III, 181.

5. Eglinton, *Irish Literary Portraits*, p. 26.

6. Moore, *Hail and Farewell*, I, 112.

7. Yeats, "The Symbolism of Poetry," *Ideas of Good and Evil*, pp. 176-177.

Dorothy Wellesley (Dorothy Wellington, Duchess of Wellesley) devotes several paragraphs in the "Comments and Conversations," appended to the collection of letters interchanged between herself and Yeats and published by Dorothy Wellesley as *Letters on Poetry*, to Yeats' lack of concern with nature. She says:

"I have come to the conclusion that this lack of 'visualness,' this lack of interest in natural beauty for its own sake, may originate in the fact that most of the Celtic poets are not concerned with nature at all. Yeats did not himself draw much inspiration from nature, certainly from no details; only sometimes massed effects, such as a painter sees, influenced his verse. Referring to a poem of mine Yeats once said to me in an outburst of irritability: 'Why can't you English poets keep flowers out of your poetry?'

"I did not reply except to point out that my reference to a 'flower' was in that particular instance quite another thing. It translated or paraphrased the old expression in folklore, referring to female fertility. I quote this to show how strongly Yeats disliked flowers, and how this lack of observation concerning natural beauty was almost an active obsession, and how it does in my opinion dim most poems of his concerned with nature. Not so with his thought.

"But there is more to say in this connexion about Yeats. I said that Celtic poetry has shown no close love or observation of nature. But of Yeats I think it is possible that to this racial characteristic must be added his extremely poor sight. His small dark eyes, turned outwards, appear like those of a lizard and as though at times they were hidden by a film. His perspective therefore is perhaps abnormal. Perhaps he cannot see very much out of doors. Certain it is that he sees nothing, when we sit together in my walled garden, in the beauty of any flower. The blossoming trees, however, interest him a little." *Letters on Poetry from W. B. Yeats to Dorothy Wellesley*, pp. 190-191.

8. Yeats, "The Happiest of the Poets," in *Ideas of Good and Evil*, p. 63.

9. Yeats, "J. M. Synge and the Ireland of His Time," *Forum*, XLVI (1911), 200.

10. Yeats, *Plays and Controversies*, p. 57.

11. Yeats, *Samhain*, Oct., 1902, p. 8.

12. Yeats, "The Symbolism of Poetry," in *Ideas of Good and Evil*, p. 167.

13. Yeats, "The Moods," in *Ideas of Good and Evil*, p. 213.

14. Yeats, "The Return of Ulysses," in *Ideas of Good and Evil*, p. 221.

15. Katharine Tynan, *The Middle Years*, p. 47.

Joseph Hone quotes a similar letter from Yeats to Edith Shackleton: "The Irish Church Gazette has given *A Vision* a long, eloquent, enthusiastic review which makes up for the stupidities of men who attribute to me some thought of their own and reply to that thought. They all think I was bound to explain myself to them. It is just that explaining which makes many English books empty." Hone, *W. B. Yeats*, p. 499.

George Moore commented on this obscurity in Yeats: ". . . and in the volume entitled *The Wind Among the Reeds* Yeats has written poems so difficult that even the adepts could not disentangle the sense" (Moore, *Hail and Farewell*, III, 179).

Notes

16. Yeats, "Symbolism in Painting," *Ideas of Good and Evil*, p. 163.
17. Yeats, "The Symbolism of Poetry," *Ideas of Good and Evil*, p. 168.
18. Yeats, *The Cutting of an Agate*, p. 46.
19. Yeats, *Collected Works*, VII, Dedication to A. E., n.p.
20. This book is generally housed as a "rare book," though published in 1939. Its rarity may possibly have been occasioned by the suppression of the book because of its Fascist views.
21. *Letters on Poetry from W. B. Yeats to Dorothy Wellesley*, pp. 182-183.
22. Yeats, "What Is Popular Poetry," in *Ideas of Good and Evil*, p. 11.
23. See Yeats, *Wheels and Butterflies*, p. 93.
24. Yeats, *Autobiography*, p. 390.
25. Strong, "W. B. Yeats," in *Scattering Branches*, p. 192.
26. A. E., *Song and Its Fountains* (London: Macmillan and Co., Ltd., 1932), pp. 9-11.
27. Yeats, *Autobiography*, p. 314.
28. *Letters on Poetry from W. B. Yeats to Dorothy Wellesley*, p. 94.
29. Yeats, *Autobiography*, p. 295.
30. *Letters on Poetry from W. B. Yeats to Dorothy Wellesley*, p. 8.
31. William Butler Yeats, Introduction, *The Oxford Book of Modern Verse* (New York: Oxford University Press, 1937), pp. xxxiv-xxxv.
32. Yeats, "The Theatre," in *Ideas of Good and Evil*, p. 179.
33. Yeats, "Literature and the Living Voice," *Contemporary Review*, XC (1906), 478.
34. *Ibid.*, p. 477.
Yeats said again: "Literature decays when it no longer makes more beautiful, or more vivid, the language which unites it to all life, and when one finds the criticism of the student, and the purpose of the reformer, and the logic of the man of science, where there should have been the reveries of the common heart ennobled into some raving Lear or unabashed Don Quixote." *The Cutting of an Agate*, p. 41.
35. Yeats, *Collected Works*, IV, 102.
36. Yeats, "Literature and the Living Voice" (see note 33, above), p. 479.
37. Quoted by Sir William Rothenstein, "Yeats as a Painter Saw Him," in *Scattering Branches*, p. 51.
38. Yeats, *Autobiography*, p. 448.
39. Yeats, "The Theatre," in *Ideas of Good and Evil*, p. 185.
40. Strong, "W. B. Yeats," in *Scattering Branches*, p. 218.
41. Yeats, "Adam's Curse," *Collected Poems*, p. 91.
42. Robinson, "The Man and the Dramatist," in *Scattering Branches*, pp. 79-80.
43. "In every edition of his [Yeats'] poems there are alterations—themselves with no air of finality—and if his poems ran through twenty editions the first version of one of his poems might hardly recognize the last. And yet Mr. Yeats' striving after the 'inevitable phrase' is apparent. Is the moral perhaps that a poet should not entertain too many ideas?" John Eglinton, "Dublin Letter," *Dial*, LXX (May, 1921), 683.
44. Yeats, *Collected Works*, Dedication to Volume VII, n.p.
45. Katharine Tynan, *Twenty-five Years*, p. 268.
46. A. E., *Some Irish Essays*, pp. 38-39.
47. *A. E.'s Letters to Mináulabáin*, p. 37.
48. *Some Passages from the Letters of A. E. to W. B. Yeats*, p. 19.
49. A. E., "The Memories of a Poet," *Irish Statesman*, VII (1926), 302.
50. Colum, "A. E.," *New Republic*, XV (1918), 173.
51. A. E. to Sean O'Casey (who had previously accused A. E. of in-

consistency), in a letter printed in *Irish Statesman,* XIII (Nov. 16, 1929), 250.

52. Yeats, *Autobiography,* p. 208.

53. Katharine Tynan, *Twenty-five Years,* p. 251.

54. A. E., *Song and Its Fountains,* p. 51.

55. A. E., "The Genius for Translation," *Irish Statesman,* III (Dec. 6, 1924), 399.

56. A. E., review of Oliver Gogarty's *An Offering of Swans,* p. 438.

57. A. E., "The Poetry of James Stephens," *Irish Statesman,* VII (Nov. 6, 1926), 205.

58. A. E., review of Yeats' *The Winding Stair, Irish Stateman,* XIII (Feb. 1, 1930), 436.

James Joyce was probably one of those who regarded spiritualism as a byway that led nowhither, for he satirized A. E.'s predilection for Eastern mysticism by burlesquing his interest: "Yogibogeybox in Dawson chambers. *Isis Unveiled.* There Palibrook we tried to pawn. Crosslegged under an umbrel umbershoot he thrones as Aztec logos, functioning on astral levels, their oversoul, mahamahatma. The faithful hermetists await the light, ripe for chelaship, ringroundabout him . . . . Filled with his God he thrones, Buddha under plantain. Gulfer of souls, engulfer. Hesouls, shesouls, shoals of souls. Engulfed with wailing creecries, whirled, whirling, they bewail" *(Ulysses,* p. 189).

59. A. E., "A Visitor from Aldebaran," *Irish Statesman,* XIII (Nov. 16, 1929), 212.

60. Stephens, "The Outlook for Literature with Special Reference to Ireland," *Century,* CIV (1922), 811.

61. Dunsany, *Patches of Sunlight,* p. 190.

62. See *Evelyn Innes,* pp. 218, 227, 304.

63. Pamela Hinkson, "Letters from W. B. Yeats," *Yale Review,* XXIX, n.s. (Dec., 1939), 320.

64. Yeats, *Wheels and Butterflies,* p. 65.

65. See Joyce, *Stephen Hero,* p. 211.

66. Eglinton, *Bards and Saints,* p. 38.

67. A. E., review of W. B. Yeats' *A Packet for Ezra Pound, Irish Statesman,* XIII (Sept. 7, 1929), 11.

68. A. E., *The Living Torch,* p. 99.

69. Colum, *The Road Round Ireland,* p. 365.

70. Strong, "John Millington Synge," *Bookman,* LXXIII (1931), 127.

71. Figgis, *Studies and Appreciations,* p. 36.

72. Stephens, "The Outlook for Literature with Special Reference to Ireland" (see note 60, above), 812.

73. Joyce, *Ulysses,* p. 210.

74. Joyce, *A Portrait of the Artist as a Young Man,* in *The Portable James Joyce,* p. 481.

75. Dodds, "Memoir," *Journal and Letters of Stephen MacKenna,* pp. 19-20.

76. George Moore, Preface to *An Anthology of Pure Poetry* (New York: Boni and Liveright, 1925), p. 18.

77. *Ibid.,* p. 43.

78. *Ibid.,* p. 17.

79. *Ibid.*

80. Moore, *Hail and Farewell,* III, 145.

81. John Millington Synge, Preface to *The Tinker's Wedding* (Dublin: Maunsel & Co., Ltd., 1907), p. vi.

82. Lady Gregory, *Our Irish Theatre,* p. 101.

83. Yeats, *Plays and Controversies,* p. 142.

Notes

84. L. A. G. Strong, "Three Irish Poets," *Commonweal*, XXII (June 7, 1935), 155.
85. John Eglinton, "Mr. Yeats' Tower," *Dial*, LXXXVI (Jan., 1929), 63.
86. Moore, *Hail and Farewell*, II, 57-58.
87. See Colum, *The Road Round Ireland*, p. 352, and Strong, "John Millington Synge" (see note 70, above), p. 132.
88. Eglinton, *Some Irish Portraits*, pp. 41-43.
89. A. E., review of *A Packet for Ezra Pound* (see note 67, above), p. 12.
90. A. E., "What Is Art?" *Irish Statesman*, III (Feb. 28, 1925), 787-788.
91. O'Connor, "Synge," in *The Irish Theatre*, p. 36.
92. Dunsany, *Patches of Sunlight*, p. 177.
93. Lady Gregory, *Our Irish Theatre*, p. 91.
94. Yeats was influenced in this direction by Gordon Craig and by his study of the Noh plays of the Japanese.
95. Ervine, *Some Impressions of My Elders*, pp. 283-284.
96. L. A. G. Strong, *Common Sense about Drama* (New York: Thomas Nelson and Sons, Ltd., 1937), p. 70.
97. Eglinton, "Yeats and his Story," *Dial*, LXXX (1926), 358.
98. L. A. G. Strong, "James Joyce and the New Fiction," *American Mercury*, XXXV (Aug., 1935), 435.
99. Joyce, *A Portrait of the Artist as a Young Man*, in *The Portable James Joyce*, p. 285.

Joyce describes his youthful enthusiasm for words in *Stephen Hero*, p. 26: "He was at once captivated by the seeming eccentricities of the prose of Freeman and William Morris. He read them as one would read a thesaurus and made a garner of the words. He read Skeat's *Etymological Dictionary* by the hour and his mind, which had from the first been only too submissive to the infant sense of wonder, was often hypnotized by the most commonplace conversation. People seemed to him strangely ignorant of the value of the words they used so glibly."

100. *Ibid.*, p. 221.
101. Eglinton, *Irish Literary Portraits*, pp. 145-146.
102. Dunsany, *Patches of Sunlight*, p. 33.
103. *Ibid.*, p. 132.
104. Eglinton, *Irish Literary Portraits*, pp. 97-98.
105. Colum, Preface to *Journal and Letters of Stephen MacKenna*, p. xvi.
106. *Some Passages from the Letters of A. E. to W. B. Yeats*, p. 26.
107. *Ibid.*, p. 4.
108. Stephen Gwynn has said: "The pure Celt is everywhere a lover and student of words and in these remote western isles, whether of Ireland or Scotland, he preserves an astonishingly rich vocabulary." *Today and Tomorrow in Ireland*, p. 22.

Chapter X

1. Robinson, "The Man and the Dramatist," in *Scattering Branches*, p. 105.
2. Padraic Colum, "Mr. Yeats's Plays and Later Poems," *Yale Review*, XIV, n.s. (Jan., 1925), 382.
3. William Butler Yeats, Preface, *Plays for an Irish Theatre* (London: A. H. Bullen, 1903), pp. vii-x.
4. Yeats, Preface, *Plays in Prose and Verse*, p. vii.
5. Of "The Pot of Broth" Yeats says in his notes to *Plays in Prose and Verse*, p. 249: "I hardly know how much of the play is my work, for Lady Gregory helped me as she has helped in every play of mine where there is dialect, and sometimes where there is not. In those first years of

the theatre we all helped one another with plots, ideas, and dialogue, but certainly I was the most indebted as I had no mastery of speech that purported to be of real life. This play may be more Lady Gregory's than mine, for I remember once urging her to include it in her own work, and her refusing to do so."

In the introduction to *Plays and Controversies*, p. vii, Yeats said: "I have sometimes asked her [Lady Gregory's] help because I could not write dialect and sometimes because my construction had fallen into confusion."

Ernest Boyd in his *Contemporary Drama of Ireland* (Boston: Little Brown and Co., 1928), p. 72, says: "*The Pot of Broth* is obviously the work of Lady Gregory rather than of Yeats, being nothing more than a trifling farce in the typical vein of her *Seven Short Plays*."

Ernest Boyd, expatriate Irish writer, long resident in the United States, was an associate member of the Irish Academy of Letters.

6. *Letters from W. B. Yeats to Dorothy Wellesley*, p. 51.

7. Yeats, Preface to *The Unicorn from the Stars*, p. ix.

8. Yeats, Preface to *Collected Plays* (New York: The Macmillan Co., 1934), n.p.

9. Yeats, *Dramatis Personae*, p. 77, or *Autobiography*, p. 386. Note that Yeats does not say "Lady Gregory with my help . . ." as he did previously, but "With Lady Gregory's help I turned it . . . ."

10. Yeats, Notes to *Plays in Prose and Verse*, p. 434.

11. N. J. O'Connor, "A Note on Yeats," in *Essays in Memory of Barrett Wendell* (Cambridge: Harvard University Press, 1926), p. 288.

12. Lady Gregory, *Our Irish Theatre*, p. 105.

13. Gogarty, *As I Was Going down Sackville Street*, pp. 282-283. Such attitudes as this of Gogarty occasioned the remark of J. B. Yeats, the father of the poet, who wrote to his daughter, Lily Yeats, in October, 1912: "It seems that Arthur Symons hates Lady Gregory and moans at mention of her . . . . Arthur Symons never speaks of her except as the 'Strega' which is the Italian for witch. I don't regret her witchcraft, though it is not easy personally to like her. They are all so prejudiced that they think her plays are all put into shape by Willie, which of course is nonsense. I for one won't turn against Lady Gregory. She is perfectly disinterested. She shows this disinterestedness. That is one of the reasons why she is infernally haughty to lesser mortals . . . ." "Letters from an Irish Painter in New York," *The Dublin Magazine*, XVI (Oct., Dec., 1941), pp. 37-38.

14. See Moore, *Hail and Farewell*, I, 282.

15. Yeats, *Autobiography*, p. 320. See also p. 349.

16. Yeats, *Collected Works*, IV, 112. See also Lady Gregory, *Our Irish Theatre*, pp. 83-84.

17. Stephen Gwynn, *Today and Tomorrow in Ireland*, p. 36.

18. Moore said in *A Communication to My Friends*, p. 83: "I found no story teller in Ireland who wished to take light from another: they all deemed that they possessed the light, and that when Ireland obtained her freedom she would rise higher than she had ever risen before; that new Ireland would rival the Greece of Pericles." The fact that Moore failed in his attempts to collaborate with Yeats and with Martyn may have influenced his general conclusion.

19. Arthur Symons complained that Lady Gregory, by drawing him over to Coole, had frustrated his lyrical vein in favor of the drama. See "Letters from an Irish Painter in New York" (see note 13, above), p. 38.

20. See Moore, *Hail and Farewell*, I, 283.

21. Yeats, *Dramatis Personae*, p. 57.

22. See Moore, *Hail and Farewell*, I, 362-363.

23. *Some Passages of A. E. to W. B. Yeats*, pp. 39-40.

Notes

24. *Ibid.*, p. 40.

25. Stephen Gwynn, "The Irish Literary Theatre and Its Affinities," *Fortnightly*, LXXVI (1901), 1057.

26. Yeats, *Autobiography*, p. 373.

27. Moore, however, speaking of *Grania and Diarmuid* in *Ideals in Ireland*, p. 45, said: ". . . It would be difficult to name any poet that Ireland has yet produced more truly elected by his individual and racial genius to interpret the old legend than the distinguished poet whose contemporary and collaborateur I have the honour to be."

28. *Samhain*, October, 1901, p. 12. On the other hand, Ernest Boyd in *The Contemporary Drama of Ireland*, p. 23, says: "It is a little difficult nowadays, when one reads the two versions, to understand why *The Tale of a Town* should have been rejected in favor of *The Bending of the Bough* which has not added anything to the reputation of George Moore. Both plays are substantially the same, although four out of five acts were rewritten in *The Bending of the Bough*."

29. Hone, *George Moore*, p. 378.

30. Yeats, *Autobiography*, p. 365.

31. *Ibid.*

32. See Denis Gwynn, *Edward Martyn*, pp. 339-340.

33. Hone, *George Moore*, p. 336.

34. Moore, *Hail and Farewell*, III, 252-253.

35. *Some Passages From the Letters of A. E. to W. B. Yeats*, p. 35.

36. Yeats, *Autobiography*, p. 383.

37. *Ibid.*

38. Moore, *Hail and Farewell*, II, 189-190.

39. Lord Dunsany is in error on this point. Lady Gregory's play, *The Deliverer*, first appeared in print in 1912 in her collection, *Folk History Plays*, II, twenty-six years before the publication of Lord Dunsany's memoirs, *Patches of Sunlight*.

40. Lord Dunsany, *Patches of Sunlight*, pp. 158-159. A comparison of the two plays does not substantiate Dunsany's claim, in my opinion.

41. Malone, "The Plays of Lady Gregory," *Yale Review*, XIV, n.s. (1925), 549.

42. Lord Dunsany, *Patches of Sunlight*, p. 155.

43. *Ibid.*, p. 189.

44. Padraic Colum said in his article, "Letter to a Young Poet," *Forum*, XCVI (Nov., 1936), x: "In the city I was brought up in there was always a poet ready to deliver the lyric he had just written to another poet, ready to listen to another, to comment on what the other had done. It is the comment made in this way that really teaches the young poet; it is from his contemporaries he learns technique and receives ideas."

45. Eglinton, *Irish Literary Portraits*, p. 24.

46. Stephen Gwynn, *Irish Literature and Drama*, p. 122.

47. Katharine Tynan, *Twenty-five Years*, p. 255.

48. Yeats said in a letter to Lady Gregory that these letters had been employed by Mrs. Hinkson (Katharine Tynan) without his permission. See Hone, *W. B. Yeats*, p. 291.

49. Katharine Tynan, *The Middle Years*, p. 36.

50. Pamela Hinkson, "Letters from W. B. Yeats," *Yale Review*, XXIX, n.s. (1939), 317-318.

51. A. E., "Yeats' Early Poetry," *Living Age*, CCCXXVII (Nov. 28, 1925), 464.

52. Yeats, "Introduction to 'Mandookya Upanishad,'" *Criterion*, XIV (1935), 548.

53. *Some Passages from the Letters of A. E. to W. B. Yeats*, p. 48.

54. Padraic Colum, "Poet's Progress," *Theater Arts Monthly,* XIX (Dec., 1935), 943.

55. Yeats, *Plays and Controversies,* p. 44.

56. St. John Ervine interprets Yeats' influence on Synge as a matter of whim rather than as logical direction. In an article, "On the Manifestations of Genius," in *Living Age,* CIV (Jan. 17, 1920), 165, Ervine said: "When Mr. Yeats advised Synge to leave Paris and go to the Aran Isles he did so, not in the belief that Synge was a dramatist of strangely individual character,—for Mr. Yeats did not then see any quality at all in Synge, —but because that was an *obiter dictum* that he would have offered to anyone who happened to be listening to him. It was simply the whim of the moment that caused Mr. Yeats to send Synge to Aran and not to Bloody Foreland Point. In another mood, Mr. Yeats might have urged him to stay in Paris!"

57. Fay, "The Poet and the Actor," in *Scattering Branches,* p. 127.

58. Yeats, "J. M. Synge and the Ireland of His Time," *Forum,* XLVI (1911), 185.

59. Dunsany, *Patches of Sunlight,* p. 154.

60. Stephen Gwynn, *Experiences of a Literary Man,* pp. 191-192.

61. Maud Gonne, "Yeats and Ireland," in *Scattering Branches,* p. 27.

62. Stephen Gwynn, *Experiences of a Literary Man,* p. 62.

63. See Lady Gregory, *Our Irish Theatre,* p. 99.

64. *Ibid.,* p. 103.

65. *Ibid.,* pp. 133-134.

66. Max Meyerfeld, "Letters of John Millington Synge," *Yale Review,* XIII, n.s. (July, 1924), 703. The letter is dated March 1, 1906.

67. In his preface to *The Unicorn from the Stars,* p. 6, Yeats said of Synge's influence on the theater: "I planned in those days to establish a dramatic movement upon the popular passions, as the ritual of religion is established in the emotions that surround birth and death and marriage, and it was only the coming of the unclassifiable, uncontrollable, capricious, uncompromising genius of J. M. Synge that altered the direction of the movement and made it individual, critical, and combative." Yeats said in his introduction to *The Oxford Book of Modern Verse,* p. xiv: "John Synge brought back masculinity to Irish verse with his harsh disillusionment, and later, when the folk movement seemed to support vague political mass excitement, certain poets began to create passionate masterful personality." Boyd, in *The Contemporary Drama of Ireland,* p. 88, said: ". . . In the main, the later dramatists derive from the tradition created by J. M. Synge and Padraic Colum." ". . . With certain exceptions, to be noted subsequently, the later 'Abbey playwrights' have contributed nothing personal to the development of the peasant play. J. M. Synge and Padraic Colum have between them prescribed the two modes of the genre, their complete dissimilarity being testimony to the original genius of each." *Ibid.,* p. 120.

68. See Hone, *W. B. Yeats,* p. 235.

69. O'Connor, "Synge," in *The Irish Theatre,* p. 37.

70. Strong, "John Millington Synge," *Bookman,* LXXIII (1931), 127. Strong later says, in *Scattering Branches,* p. 197: "He [Yeats] had always this mark of the great artist, that he could surrender to an influence, and emerge from it more strongly himself than ever. Blake, Shelley, Ferguson, Douglas Hyde, Standish O'Grady, the French symbolists, Lady Gregory, Synge, Ezra Pound—he found in them all something that belonged to him and helped him to fulfilment."

71. *Some Passages from the Letters of A. E. to W. B. Yeats,* p. 51.

72. Moore, *Hail and Farewell,* II, 87.

Notes

73. Diarmuid Russell, "A. E.," *Atlantic Monthly*, CLXXI (Feb., 1943), 53.

74. Stephen Gwynn, *Irish Literature and Drama*, p. 136.

75. *Ibid.*, p. 120.

76. Frank O'Connor, "Two Friends: Yeats and A. E.," *Yale Review*, XXIX, n.s. (1939), 60.

77. Lord Dunsany, *My Ireland*, p. 7.

78. N. J. O'Connor, "A Note on Yeats," in *Essays in Memory of Barrett Wendell*, p. 288.

79. Quoted by Katharine Tynan in *Years of the Shadow*, p. 296.

80. Pamela Hinkson, "Letters from W. B. Yeats" (see note 50, above), p. 317.

81. Moore, *Hail and Farewell*, I, 87.

82. Colum, "The Promise of Irish Letters," *Nation*, CXVII (1923), 397. Moore said in "A Dedication to Robert Ross," in *A Mummer's Wife*, p. viii: "To live for five and twenty years is as long an immortality as anyone should set his heart on for who would wish to be chattered about by people that will live in these islands three hundred years hence? We should not understand them nor they us . . . . Let us be content, Ross, to be remembered by our friends, and, perhaps, to have our names passed on by disciples to another generation."

83. Ervine, *Some Impressions of My Elders*, p. 183.

84. Padraic Colum, "Irish Poetry," *Bookman*, LIV (Oct., 1920), 115.

85. Colum, "Dr. Hyde of Eire," *Commonweal*, XXX (1939), 147.

86. Malone, "The Rise of the Realistic Movement," in *The Irish Theatre*, p. 99.

87. Strong, "James Joyce and the New Fiction," *American Mercury*, XXXV (1935), 437.

88. Stephen Gwynn, *Irish Literature and Drama*, p. 200.

89. John Eglinton, "Dublin Letter," *Dial*, LXXIII (Oct., 1922), 437.

90. Ernest Boyd, "Joyce and the New Irish Writers," *Current History*, XXXIX (March, 1934), 700.

91. Ernest Boyd, review of Sean O'Casey's *Pictures in the Hallway*, *The Saturday Review of Literature*, XXV (March 21, 1942), 5.

BIBLIOGRAPHY

Books

A. E. See Russell, George W.

A. E.'s Letters to Mindnlabáin, edited by Lucy Kingsley Porter. New York: The Macmillan Co., 1937.

An Anthology of Pure Poetry, edited by George Moore. New York: Boni and Liveright, 1925.

Boyd, Ernest A. *The Contemporary Drama of Ireland.* Boston: Little, Brown and Co., 1917.

Colum, Padraic. *The Road Round Ireland.* New York: The Macmillan Co., 1926.

Corkery, Daniel. *Synge and Anglo-Irish Literature.* Cork University Press, 1931.

Duff, Charles. *James Joyce and the Plain Reader.* London: D. Harmsworth, 1932.

Dunsany, Lord. *My Ireland.* London and New York: Funk and Wagnalls Co., 1937.

Patches of Sunlight. New York: Reynal and Hitchcock, 1938.

Eglinton, John. *Bards and Saints.* Dublin; Maunsel and Co., Ltd., 1906.

Anglo-Irish Essays. New York: John Lane Co., 1918.

Irish Literary Portraits. London: Macmillan and Co., Ltd., 1935.

Ervine, St. John. *Some Impressions of My Elders.* New York: Macmillan Co., 1922.

The Organized Theatre. New York: The Macmillan Co., 1924.

Essays in Memory of Barrett Wendell. Cambridge: Harvard University Press, 1926.

Figgis, Darrell. *Studies and Appreciations.* London: J. M. Dent Sons, Ltd., 1912.

A. E. (George W. Russell), A Study of a Man and a Nation. Dublin: Maunsel and Co., Ltd., 1916.

Gogarty, Oliver St. John. *As I Was Going down Sackville Street.* London: Rich and Cowan, Ltd., 1937.

I Follow St. Patrick. New York: Reynal and Hitchcock, 1938.

Going Native. New York: Duell, Sloan and Pearce, 1940.

Gorman, Herbert. *James Joyce.* New York: Farrar and Rinehart, Inc., 1939.

Gregory, Lady Augusta. *Our Irish Theatre.* New York and London: G. P. Putnam's Sons, 1913.

The Kiltartan Poetry Book. New York and London: G. P. Putnam's Sons, 1919.

Gwynn, Denis. *Edward Martyn and the Irish Revival.* London: Jonathan Cape, 1930.

Gwynn, Stephen. *Today and Tomorrow in Ireland.* Dublin: Hodges, Figgis and Co., Ltd., 1903.

Experiences of a Literary Man. New York: Henry Holt and Co., 1927.

Irish Literature and Drama. London and New York: Thomas Nelson and Sons, Ltd., 1936.

Hone, Joseph. *The Life of George Moore.* London: V. Gollancz, 1936.

W. B. Yeats. New York: The Macmillan Co., 1943.

Ideals in Ireland, edited by Lady Gregory. London: At the Unicorn VII Cecil Court, 1901.

Joyce, James. *A Portrait of the Artist as a Young Man.* New York: Random House, The Modern Library Edition, 1928.

Bibliography

Anna Livia Plurabelle. New York: Crosby Gaige, 1928.
Ulysses. New York: Random House, Modern Library Edition, 1934.
Stephen Hero. New York: New Directions Press, 1944.
Law, H. A. *Anglo-Irish Literature.* New York: Longmans, Green and Co., Ltd., 1926.
Letters on Poetry from W. B. Yeats to Dorothy Wellesley, edited by Dorothy Wellesley. London: Oxford University Press, 1940.
MacKenna, Stephen. *Journal and Letters of Stephen MacKenna,* edited by E. R. Dodds. New York: W. Morrow and Co., 1937.
Malone, A. E. *The Irish Drama.* London: Constable and Co., Ltd., 1929.
Martyn, Edward. *The Heather Field.* London: Duckworth and Co., 1899.
The Dream Physician. New York: Brentano's, 1918.
Mitchell, Susan. *George Moore.* New York: Dodd, Mead and Co., 1916.
Moore, George. *Evelyn Innes.* New York and London: D. Appleton and Co., 1915.
A Mummer's Wife. London: Wm. Heinemann, 1918.
Hail and Farewell, 3 vols. New York and London: The Macmillan Co., 1924.
A Communication to My Friends. London: The Nonesuch Press, 1933.
Russell, George (A. E.). *Some Irish Essays.* Dublin: Maunsel and Co., Ltd., 1906.
Song and Its Fountains. London: Macmillan and Co., Ltd., 1932.
The National Being. New York: The Macmillan Co., 1937.
The Living Torch. New York: The Macmillan Co., 1938.
Samhain. (See Yeats, *Plays and Controversies,* in this bibliography.)
Scattering Branches; Tributes to the Memory of W. B. Yeats, edited by Stephen Gwynn. New York: The Macmillan Co., 1940.
Shaw, George Bernard. *John Bull's Other Island.* London: Constable and Co., 1928.
Some Passages from the Letters of A. E. to W. B. Yeats. Dublin: The Cuala Press, 1936.
Strong, L. A. G. *Common Sense About Drama.* New York: Thomas Nelson and Sons, Ltd., 1937.
Synge, John Millington. *The Tinker's Wedding.* London: Maunsel and Co., 1907.
Synge, Samuel. *Letters to My Daughter.* Dublin and Cork: The Talbot Press, Ltd., 1932.
The Irish Home Rule Convention. New York: The Macmillan Co., 1917.
The Irish Theatre, edited by Lennox Robinson. London: Macmillan and Co., Ltd., 1939.
The New International Yearbook, 1945.
The Oxford Book of Modern Verse, edited by W. B. Yeats. New York: Oxford University Press, 1937.
The Statesman's Yearbook, 1944.
Tynan, Katharine (Mrs. Hinkson). *Twenty-five Years.* London: Smith, Elder and Co., 1913.
The Middle Years. London: Constable and Co., Ltd., 1916.
The Years of the Shadow. London: Constable and Co., Ltd., 1919.
Collected Poems. London: Macmillan and Co., Ltd., 1930.
Yeats, William Butler. *The Celtic Twilight.* London: A. H. Bullen, 1902.
Plays for An Irish Theatre. London: A. H. Bullen, 1903.
Collected Works. Stratford-on-Avon. The Shakespeare Head Press, 1908.
The Unicorn from the Stars. New York: The Macmillan Co., 1908.
The Cutting of An Agate. New York: The Macmillan Co., 1912.
Ideas of Good and Evil. London: A. H. Bullen, 1914.

The Modern Irish Writers

Plays and Controversies. London: Macmillan and Co., Ltd., 1923. This includes Yeats' contribution to *Samhain,* an occasional publication started in the third year of the Irish dramatic movement, to defend that movement.

Plays in Prose and Verse. New York: The Macmillan Co., 1928.

Collected Plays. New York: The Macmillan Co., 1934.

The King of the Great Clock Tower, Commentaries and Poems. New York: The Macmillan Co., 1935.

Wheels and Butterflies. New York: The Macmillan Co., 1935.

Dramatis Personae. New York: The Macmillan Co., 1936.

The Collected Poems of W. B. Yeats. New York: The Macmillan Co., 1940.

Autobiography. New York: The Macmillan Co., 1943.

Articles

A. E. See Russell, George W.

Archer, William. "Real Conversations," *Critic,* XXXIX (1901), 47-56.

Boyd, Ernest. "Joyce and the New Irish Writers," *Current History,* XXXIX (1934), 699-704.

Review of Sean O'Casey's *Pictures in the Hallway, Saturday Review of Literature,* XXV (1942), 5.

Colum, Mary. "Shaw and Synge," *Forum,* XCIV (1935), 357-358.

"Lady Gregory and the Abbey Theater," *Tomorrow,* IV (1945), 20-24.

Colum, Padraic. "The Irish Literary Movement,"*Forum,* LIII (1915), 133-148.

"A. E.," *New Republic,* XV (1918), 172-174.

"Irish Poetry," *Bookman,* LIV (1920), 109-115.

"The Promise of Irish Letters," *Nation,* CXVII (1923), 396-397.

"Mr. Yeats's Plays and Later Poems," *Yale Review,* XIV, n.s. (1925), 381-385.

"Dublin in Literature," *Bookman,* LXIII (1926), 556-561.

"Ulysses in its Epoch," *Saturday Review of Literature,* X (1934), 433, 438.

"Poet's Progress," *Theater Arts Monthly,* XIX (1935), 936-943.

"Dr. Hyde of Eire," *Commonweal,* XXX (1939), 146-148.

"Oliver Gogarty on James Joyce," *Saturday Review of Literature,* XXIII (1941), 11.

"Letter to a Young Poet," *Forum,* XCVI (1936), 240, x.

Cumberland, Gerald. "The Amazing Dubliners," *Century,* CI (1921), 311-316.

Desmond, Shaw. "Dunsany, Yeats, and Shaw," *Bookman,* LVIII (1923), 260-266.

Eglinton, John. "The Modern Irishman and the Mere Irishman," *Living Age,* CCXCI (1916), 425-428.

"Dublin Letter," *Dial,* LXX (1921), 682-685.

"Dublin Letter," *Dial,* LXXII (1922), 619-622.

"Dublin Letter," *Dial,* LXXIII (1922), 434-437.

"Yeats and His Story," *Dial,* LXXX (1926), 357-366.

"George Moore and Holy Ireland," *Dial,* LXXXVI (1929), 339-343.

"Irish Letter," *Dial,* LXXXVI (1929), 417-420.

"Mr. Yeats' Tower," *Dial,* LXXXVI (1929), 62-65.

Ellis, Havelock, "The Celtic Spirit in Literature," *Living Age,* CCXLVIII (1906), 579-590.

Bibliography

Ervine, St. John. "On the Manifestations of Genius,"*Living Age*, CCCIV (1920), 165-168.

Feld, R. C. "The Opinions of A. E.," *Century*, CIII (1921), 3-9.

Gogarty, Oliver St. John. "Next Door to George Moore," *Saturday Review of Literature*, XIV (1936), 3-4.

Gwynn, Stephen. "The Irish Literary Theatre and Its Affinities," *Fortnightly*, LXXVI (1901), 1050-1062.

"Ebb and Flow," *Fortnightly*, CXLIV, n.s. (1938), 739-744.

Hinkson, Pamela. "Letters from W. B. Yeats," *Yale Review*, XXIX, n.s. (1939), 307-320. *W. B. Yeats' Letters to Katharine Tynan*, edited by Roger McHugh, were published by McMullen Books, Inc., New York, 1953.

Joyce, James, "Ibsen's New Drama," *Fortnightly Review*, LXXIII (1900), 575-590.

Kelleher, John V. "Irish Literature Today," *Atlantic Monthly*, CLXXV (1945), 70-76.

"Letters from an Irish Painter in New York," *Dublin Magazine, A Quarterly Review*, XVI (1941), 34-44.

"Literary Notes," *Dublin Penny Journal* (April 5, 1902), 5. This gathering carries no volume number.

Malone, A. E. "The Plays of Lady Gregory," *Yale Review*, XIV, n.s. (1925), 540-551.

Meyerfeld, Max, "Letters of John Millington Synge,"*Yale Review*, XIII, n.s. (1924), 690-709.

Moore, George. "A Plea for the Soul of the Irish People," *Nineteenth Century*, LXIX (1901), 285-295.

O'Connor, Frank. "Two Friends: Yeats and A. E.," *Yale Review*, XXIX, n.s. (1939), 60-88.

Ratcliffe, S. K. "George Moore's Burial," *Nation*, CXXVI (1933), 205-206.

Russell, Diarmuid. "A. E.," *Atlantic*, CLXXI (1943), 51-57.

Russell, George (A. E.). "Irish Anticipations," *Survey*, XLVII (1921), 291-294.

Review of Oliver Gogarty's *An Offering of Swans*, *Irish Statesman*, I (1923), 436-438.

Review of Padraic Colum's *Castle Conquer*, *Irish Statesman*, I (1923), 116.

Review of James Stephens' *In the Land of Youth*, *Irish Statesman*, III (1924), 278-280.

"Yeats' Early Poetry," *Living Age*, CCCXXVII (1925), 464-466.

"What is Art?" *Irish Statesman*, III (1925), 787-789.

"The Memories of a Poet," *Irish Statesman*, VII (1926), 399-400.

"The Poetry of James Stephens," *Irish Statesman*, VII (1926), 399-400.

"Anglo-Irish Literature," *Irish Statesman*, VII (1927), 477-478.

Review of W. B. Yeats' *A Packet for Ezra Pound*, *Irish Statesman*, XIII (1929), 11-12.

"A Visitor from Aldebaran," *Irish Statesman*, XIII (1929), 212-216.

Letter to Sean O'Casey, "Correspondence," *Irish Statesman*, XIII (1929), 250-251.

Review of Yeats' *The Winding Stair*, *Irish Statesman*, XIII (1930), 436-437.

"The Genius for Translation," *Irish Statesman*, III (1942), 399-400.

Stephens, James. "Dublin," *Living Age*, CIV (1920), 168-171.

"The Outlook for Literature with Special Reference to Ireland," *Century*, CIV (1922), 811-818.

"Irish Letter," *Dial*, LXXVI (1924), 523-526.

169

The Modern Irish Writers

Strong, L. A. G. "John Millington Synge," *Bookman*, LXXIII (1931), 125-136.

"Three Irish Poets," *Commonweal*, XXII (1935), 433-437.

"James Joyce and the New Fiction," *American Mercury*, XXXV (1935), 433-437.

Yeats, W. B. "Literature and the Living Voice," *Contemporary Review*, XC (1906), 472-482.

"J. M. Synge and the Ireland of his Time,"*Forum*, XLVI (1911), 179-200.

"More Memories," *Dial*, LXXIII (1922), 48-72; 133-158; 395-410.

"The Need for Audacity of Thought," *Dial*, LXXX (1926), 115-119.

"Introduction to 'Mandookya Upanishad,' " *Criterion*, XIV (1935), 547-558.

INDEX

Abbey Theatre, writers connected with, 8; conflict over founding of, 10; players' acting powers, 12; development from National Theatre Society, 15; accomplishment, 20; plays of, 119

Academy of Letters, evidence of a conscious school of writers, 21; Yeats' idea, 21; A. E.'s distrust of, 21; inclusive nature of, 21; formation of, 21

A. E. (George Russell) one of central coterie, 8; recognition of his leadership, 10; Gaelic legends as symbols, 16; distrust of Academy, 21; protests pronouncement of extinction of Irish literary school, 22; devotion to Ireland, 26; urges Frank O'Connor to remain in Ireland, 26; horror of London, 27; on the province of national literature, 32-33; evaluation of by Lord Dunsany, 33-34; criticized for taint of sentimentality, 34; disapproves excesses of Republicans, 42; advocate of Home Rule, 42; support of Gaelic revival limited, 56-58, 62-63; compared to Plato, 66; compares Gogarty's lyrics with Greek anthology, 67; compared to Leonardo da Vinci, 68; compared to Shakespeare, 68; compares Colum to Turgenieff, 71; draws analogy between Irish and ancient Greeks, 72; defines a literary movement, 73; unanimously admired, 73; personal appearance of, 73, 76-77, 78; complains of Yeats' aloofness, 82; his discovery of James Stephens, 87-88; Moore's damaging insinuation, 89; Moore's devotion to, 89; quarrel with Moore, 89-90; subject of fictionalized portraits, 90-91; his deep regard for MacKenna, 102; fundamental concepts in harmony with those of Yeats, 110-13; his theory of race-memory, 112; his mysticism, 112-13; sees psychic energy in fellow members of Irish school, 113; emphasis on personal mystic experience, 114; shares Yeats' attitude toward factual description of na-

ture, 118; no ascetic, 119; discusses word values with Yeats, 123; advises Moore to drop collaboration, 130; accuses Moore of plagiarism, 132; opposes Yeats' plan for American tour of Abbey company, 135; attempt at anonymity, 138; his involuntary influence, 138-39, 141; approves Katharine Tynan, 144; longing for Ireland, 146; dislike of America, 146-47; his Orientalism, 148; practical concern with co-operatives, 154

Anglo-Irish, literature assessed, 3; literature contrasted with Irish literature, 15; defined, 38; foster Irish dislike of the English, 45; called the salt of the earth, 47; dialects employed, 58

Boyd, Ernest A., connection with central coterie, 8; discounts Joyce's influence, 141; attributes *Pot of Broth* to Lady Gregory, 162; calls Synge progenitor of new drama, 164

Colum, Mary, compares Synge with Greek dramatists, 65; on Lady Gregory, 157

Colum, Padraic, criticism of Irish writers in *The Road Round Ireland*, 3; recognition of the coterie, 7; connection with central coterie, 8; on loss of Synge, 20; acknowledges breakup of coterie, 22-23; attitude toward revival of Gaelic, 58-59; attributes vast powers to A. E., 67; declares Joyce's lyrics equal to Elizabethan, 69; compared to Turgenieff, 71; compared to Blake, 118; on influence of Lady Gregory on Yeats, 124; suggests theme for Dunsany play, 133; inspired by Dublin players, 136; finds Moore's novels negligible as a literary influence, 140; as initiator of realistic movement, 140; on camaraderie among the poets, 163; on literary immortality, 165

Coole, copper-beech register, 8; as a Minstrelburg, 14; Synge at home

171

Index

failure to understand the Irish peasant, 38; interest in politics, 44-45; edits *Ideals in Ireland*, 51-52; attitude toward revival of Gaelic, 58; compared with Malory and Welsh authors, 71; personal appearance of, 76; George Moore's dislike of, 91; attitude toward youthful Joyce, 97-98; aversion to propaganda plays, 117; *Our Irish Theatre*, 119-20; influence on Yeats, 124; collaboration with Yeats, 125-28; accused by Dunsany of borrowing his plot, 132-33; her play, *The Deliverer*, called atypical, 133; defines Celtic Movement, 143; Symons' dislike of, 162

Griffith, Arthur, his interest in Gaelic, 48

Gwynn, Denis, connection with central coterie, 8; champion of Edward Martyn, 10; denounces Lady Gregory, 11

Gwynn, Stephen, connection with central coterie, 8; his comment on Katharine Tynan, 8; holds "stage-Irishman" to be legitimate caricature, 17; returns yearly to Ireland, 27-28; defines the Irish character, 38-39; notes Yeats' arrogance, 79; his interpretation of codicil of Martyn's will, 131

Hackett, Francis, attitude toward the English, 46

Higgins, F. R., notes Yeats' contempt for "Middle minds," 82

Hone, Joseph, indicates inclusive nature of Academy, 21-22; cites Hyde as creator of Gaelic League, 50-51; accents Yeats' aloofness, 80-81; says Moore's social life not curtailed, 95; on Moore's collaborations, 131

Hyde, Douglas, connection with central coterie, 8; connections centered in Gaelic League, 13; refuses invitation to Academy, 22; his Celtic appearance, 34-35; paradoxical situation of, 47; his *Literary History of Ireland*, 48; propagandizes for revival of Gaelic, 48; founder of Gaelic League, 49-51; denials of claims as founder, 50; Moore's description of him speaking Gaelic, 54; compared to Musset and Banville, 69; personal appearance of, 75, 77; indebted to Yeats and Lady Gregory, 129; his literary influence, 140

Ibsen, Henrik, Joyce talks of, 9; Yeats' praise of, 19

Ideals in Ireland, 150

Irish Academy of Letters, a center of the coterie, 7

Irish Literary Theatre, statement of purpose, 18

Irish Literary Revival, as English revival conducted by Irishmen, 10

Irish National Literary Society, denounces propagandist verse, 15; denial of pseudo-patriotism, 16; forerunner of the Abbey Theatre, 17

Joyce, James, his aloofness from central coterie, 9; talks of Ibsen, 9; sees no reason for his invitation to Academy, 22; his expatriation foreshadowed, 24; disgusted by scruples of Dublin publishers, 24; his objectivity, 24; his attitude toward revival of Gaelic, 60-61; referred to as Dublin's Dante, 67; personal appearance of, 67, 73; describes appearances of Dublin writers, 78; his attitude toward Lady Gregory and Yeats, 97-98; his attitude toward Gogarty, 99-100; on subjectivity of the artist, 115; *Finnegans Wake*, 116; austerity of, 118; his exaltation of the word, 121, 161; his influence, 140-42; juxtaposes in *Ulysses* names of Dublin coterie, 143-44; burlesques A. E.'s Eastern mysticism, 160

Kelleher, John V., pronounces extinction of Irish School of literature, 22

MacKenna, Stephen, connection with central coterie, 8; refusal of invitation to Academy, 22; attitude toward revival of Gaelic, 58; his close knowledge of Synge, 101-2; visited by George Moore, 102; influenced by Yeats' theory of the mask, 115-16; his exaltation of the word, 122; translator of Plotinus, 151

173

Index